The Fabian Society

The Fabian Society is Britain' tank and political society, com ideas and policy debates wh progressive politics.

D0130387

With over 300 Fabian MPs, MEPs, Peers, MSPs and AMs, the Society plays an unparalleled role in linking the ability to influence policy debates at the highest level with vigorous grassroots debate among our growing membership of over 7000 people, 70 local branches meeting regularly throughout Britain and a vibrant Young Fabian section organising its own activities. Fabian publications, events and ideas therefore reach and influence a wider audience than those of any comparable think tank. The Society is unique among think tanks in being a thriving, democratically-constituted membership organisation, affiliated to the Labour Party but organisationally and editorially independent.

For over 120 years Fabians have been central to every important renewal and revision of left of centre thinking. The Fabian commitment to open and participatory debate is as important today as ever before as we explore the ideas, politics and policies which will define the next generation of progressive politics in Britain, Europe and around the world. To find out more about the Fabian Society, the Young Fabians, the Fabian Women's Network and our local societies, please visit our web site at **www.fabians.org.uk**.

Joining the Fabians is easy
For more information about joining the Fabian Society and to learn more about our recent publications, please turn to **page 123**.

The Change We Need

*What Britain can learn from
Obama's victory*

Edited by Nick Anstead and Will Straw

"Change will not come if we wait for some other person or some other time. We are the ones we've been waiting for. We are the change we seek."

Barack Obama,
5th February 2008, Chicago

Fabian Society
11 Dartmouth Street
London SW1H 9BN
www.fabians.org.uk

Editorial Director: Tom Hampson
Editorial Manager: Ed Wallis

A Fabian Special
First published 2009
ISBN 978 0 7163 4107 9

British Library Cataloguing in Publication data.
A catalogue record for this book is available from the British Library.

Printed and bound by DG3

We would especially like to thank the Dartmouth Street Trust for their generous support.

Contents

Figures and tables

Acknowledgements

The editors would like to thank Jessica Asato, David Boyle, Matt Browne, Andrew Chadwick, Josh Dorner, Claire Howard, Hannah Jameson, Sadiq Khan, Declan McHugh, Kirsty McNeill, David Radloff, Phil Riley, Mark Rusling, Tom Stoate, Jack Straw and Rob Vance who have all, both directly and indirectly, influenced this pamphlet. Also, our thanks goes to our many colleagues at the Center for American Progress, Royal Holloway and the University of East Anglia, as well as our friends in the Labour Party and wider progressive movement, who have all been so important in helping foment the ideas that drove the development of this volume. Additionally, we are grateful to Rodrigo Davies for his copy-editing skills and sharpening up our original text.

We are deeply indebted to Sunder Katwala, Tom Hampson, Ed Wallis, and Rachael Jolley at the Fabian Society whose hard work and expertise made this volume possible.

Last, but not least, we are grateful to all the authors of the chapters in this pamphlet, many of whom produced their work at very short notice.

Contributors

Editors

Nick Anstead is a lecturer in politics at the University of East Anglia. His research is focused largely on parties, new political communication, and civic participation. He has appeared on national television and radio to discuss his work and blogs at nickanstead.com/blog. Nick can be contacted at nick.anstead@gmail.com.

Will Straw is Associate Director for Economic Growth at the Center for American Progress and writes for ProgressOnline, LabourList and Comment is Free. He can be contacted at willstraw@gmail.com.

Authors

Ben Brandzel is a Founding Advisor for 38 Degrees which is launching this spring at www.38degrees.org.uk. He was the North Carolina Online Campaign Director for Barack Obama, served as the Advocacy Director of MoveOn.org, and has worked for many online and offline organizing efforts around the world.

Gordon Brown has been Prime Minister of the United Kingdom since 2007. He is MP for Kirkcaldy and Cowdenbeath and has been a member of the Fabian Society since 1986.

Karin Christiansen was an Obama volunteer in the primary elections in New York State Headquarters and the general election in the Virginia Beach Office.

Robert Gerber was an advisor to Glenn Nye during the 2008 congressional election and works as a foreign affairs professional in Washington.

Yair Ghitza is a PhD student in Political Science at Columbia University. He previously worked for political analysis firms including Catalist and Copernicus Analytics.

Kate Kenski is an Assistant Professor at the University of Arizona where she teaches political communication and research methods. She is also a research consultant for the National Annenberg Election Survey. Kenski is a co-author of the book *Capturing Campaign Dynamics: The National Annenberg Election Survey* and has published articles and research notes in a number of academic journals.

David Lammy is the Labour MP for Tottenham and the Minister of State for Innovation, Universities and Skills. During the 2008 American elections he spent time with the Obama campaign in Chicago and in contested primary states.

Matthew McGregor is the Director of the London Office of Blue State Digital – the organisation that built Obama's social network MyBO. As well as working on campaigns in the US, France and Sweden, he organised Jon Cruddas's Deputy Leadership campaign in 2006-7, and worked for Ken Livingstone's 2008 Mayoral bid. He has also been employed by trade justice advocates War on Want and the TULO, the coalition of Labour supporting trade unions.

Glenn Nye is in his first term as Democratic member of the US House of Representatives for Virginia's 2nd Congressional District. He won his seat in November 2008 by defeating two-term Republican incumbent Thelma Drake.

Marcus Roberts was an Obama Volunteer Organiser in Ohio. Previously he lost the Gore 2000, Carnahan 2002, Kerry 2004 and Madrid 2006 elections. He is now a happy man.

Todd Rogers is the Executive Director of the Analyst Institute, which assists progressive organisations to use randomised controlled experiments and data-driven innovations in politics. He received his PhD from Harvard Business School and the Harvard Psychology Department.

Faiz Shakir is the Research Director at the Center for American Progress and serves as Editor-in-Chief of ThinkProgress.org. He holds a BA degree in Government from Harvard University and a JD degree from the Georgetown Law Center.

Robert Y Shapiro is the Professor of Political Science and Acting Director, Institute for Social and Economic Research and Policy, Columbia University. He is the author of *Politicians Don't Pander: Political Manipulation and the Loss of Democratic Responsiveness* with Lawrence R Jacobs.

Jennifer Stromer-Galley is an Assistant Professor in the Department of Communication at the University at Albany, SUNY. Her research focuses on the political uses of new communication technology, including political blogging, presidential campaigning through the internet, and citizen's political talk.

Foreword
Rt Hon Gordon Brown MP

We tend to think of the sweep of destiny as stretching across many months and years – as if each minute leads inevitably to the next, before culminating in decisive moments we call history. But sometimes the defining moments of history appear suddenly and with no warning, and the task of leadership is to name them, shape them and move forward into the new world they help to create.

I think we are in one of those moments now. An economic hurricane has spread across the world and lashed our shores and only progressive values hold the answer to it. When I travel around Britain I sense a real hunger for the economic change Labour is fighting for and for the co-operative solutions that can make the fair society real in our generation.

And so this is a good time to reflect on how our Labour Party can better serve the interests of Britain. This book reminds us of what we all know, but sometimes forget to articulate clearly: that people join progressive parties not just to help them win elections, but to help them win the change their countries need.

Contained within these pages are the ideas of tomorrow – the new ways of working that will help Labour members do even more to change our world. It contains fascinating accounts from people who have held senior leadership positions across American professional politics, but what comes through most clearly is that they never felt the

Obama campaign was primarily about hiring the best full-timers. Rather, this was people-powered politics, an exercise in harnessing the talents and enthusiasm of so-called ordinary people.

The stunning success of the campaign in recruiting, retaining and deploying volunteers was not just a model of political organising, but a profound political ideal in itself. At the core of it was the idea that every single person is both precious and unique, each born endowed with a contribution only they can make. At each level and stage of the campaign the organising principle was the same: the purpose of politics is to help people bridge the gap between what they are and what they have it within themselves to become.

It reminded me of that brilliant video that was made for Live 8. It shows great social movements in history – but it pans past the people who made the headlines and focuses in on the people behind them. So in the mass abolitionist rallies it goes past Wilberforce to focus on a face in the crowd. Then they show the votes for women campaign and go past the Pankhursts to those who protested alongside them. And then it shows the march on Washington but pans past Dr King to focus on all those he had mobilised to march with him.

The point it makes, of course, is that winning progressive battles is not just about who leads – but about who commits and dedicates their lives to the struggle. Great change is only won and sustained when leaders inspire others to follow – when they stand up for justice and pass its torch along, person to person, to build a movement, first hundreds, then thousands and then finally millions strong.

The Obama campaign stood in that long and noble tradition of movement-based politics. Our own Labour Party also has that strain in our inheritance. As a grand coming together of trade unionists and Fabians and co-operators and Christian socialists, latterly embracing the tenants' movement and the campaigners for gay and women's and black equality, ours was never intended to be a rigid and brittle party structure.

So we need to remember that great responsibility rests on our shoulders not just as a government but as a party. If we are to continue being the change that Britain needs we must always remember that we are more than a home for tribal political loyalties; that our Labour family is a movement inspired by a calling to which all people of good conscience can rally.

I have recently returned from America where I met with politicians, journalists and activists. What was clear from each was just how enthused people had become through a campaign once written off as a long-shot insurgency. We should all be inspired by the success of those whose success is down simply to their courage in willing it.

The road ahead is a hard one, but we should travel with confidence, because the momentum of history is not towards the right. The pendulum is swinging to the centre-left, to the people who believe that while markets should be free they should never be values-free, and that doing what is fair matters more than being *laissez-faire*.

Progressives have never been better placed to win the battle of ideas. This timely book shows us how we might adapt some lessons that would enable us to win the battle of organisation too. Each requires a ruthless focus on effective collaboration and a celebration of the idea that we achieve more working with others than we ever could alone.

So let us say to those who have disengaged, to those once on our side who have given up hope, let us say and mean what has always been true and which this recent American election has done so much to illuminate: those who stand for progress stand together.

1. Introduction
Nick Anstead and Will Straw

The 2008 American election was not just business as usual and it marked a significant break from the past. Cynics will argue that Barack Obama's message of 'hope' and 'change' was just rhetoric, and he certainly could not have asked for better circumstances in which to face the Republicans. But Obama ultimately prevailed because he embodied the messages he was preaching.

He was, of course, the first African-American to win either party's nomination. His speech on race in March 2008 did much to address the fears of those who worried that his campaign might be framed by anger or bitterness. His eloquent argument that "we perfect our union by understanding that we may have different stories, but we hold common hopes," and his own tale – detailed in *Dreams From My Father*, – as the son of a black man from Kenya and a white woman from Kansas underscored his ideas and forged a new approach to politics.[1] He advocated an end to partisan division, the shattering of Washington's entrenched vested interests, and a pragmatic style that asked what works, not where the idea came from.

Obama also symbolised generational change, as he was the first post-Vietnam War presidential candidate. This was a hugely significant shift as, for more than two decades, the war and the divisions it had created in the US provided the background against which elections were fought. Candidates' service records, accusations of draft dodging and the intervention of organisations like the Swift Boat

Veterans proved decisive in election after election. Obama, though, was just three years old when the Tonkin Bay Incident led to President Johnson escalating American involvement in Vietnam. Because he was from a different generation, Obama was able to transcend the culture wars that had dominated American politics since Nixon's victory in 1968. Unlike Kerry or Gore before him, he avoided getting bogged down in issues like abortion, gun control, or gay rights, and instead focused relentlessly on his judgment over the Iraq War and, later, his plans to revive the ailing economy.

Just as his race, age, and policies signified change, so too did his campaign. Elections are frequently defined by specific innovations. The 1960 election, for example, will be forever remembered for the contrast in the first televised debate between a youthful and photogenic John F Kennedy, and a pale and unshaven Richard Nixon (who was just four years his senior). The 2008 election will be remembered for Obama's mastery of the internet.

As the chapters in this book detail, Obama's network of supporters were mobilised in an unparalleled manner through the most technically sophisticated campaign of all time. Activists used the social networking feature on his web site, my.barackobama.com, to organise voter-registration drives and canvassing operations. Data was used with ever increasing sophistication to enhance the efficiency of all aspects of campaigning, and was quickly converted from the clipboard to mainframe computers in Chicago. The Obama campaign raised an unprecedented $657 million in donations from supporters, of which more than $500 million was given online. And in the blogosphere, the netroots community undertook a relentless rebuttal operation against John McCain, Sarah Palin and President Bush, providing endless material for the mainstream media.

This book documents this story, asking at every stage what lessons are applicable to Britain and specifically to Obama's ideological bed fellows, the Labour Party. With a British general election due at some point in the next fifteen months, the timing could not be more apposite. When it comes, the election campaign will be the most fiercely competitive in nearly a generation. And with the global economy in peril, the stakes could not be higher.

To be clear, we do not argue that Obama's campaign strategies can be imported wholesale from the United States or simply emulated through replication. To attempt to do so would be to ignore the considerable institutional, cultural and circumstantial differences between American and British politics. We do, however, believe that for every aspect of the American election – grassroots mobilisation, volunteer management, the use of data, blogging, and even fundraising – there are lessons that the Labour Party must absorb. Failure to do so will give the Conservative Party a strategic advantage when every vote counts more than at any time since the nail biter in 1992.

While these lessons and the recommendations that flow from them form the change we need, it will not be easy. The Party must adapt its culture in order to capitalise on these innovations. Labour's winning formula over the last decade of centralised command and control is at odds with the defining characteristics of the early 21st century. Society is more fragmented, atomised and diverse than ever before, yet individuals – particularly the young – use the networks of Facebook and MySpace to replicate the community spirit of old. Much of what Obama achieved was only possible because of the openness with which he ran his campaign and the decentralisation of key tasks to his myriad supporters. Such an approach is alien to the modern Labour Party.

We argue that Obama's victory shows that the Party no longer has to choose between being, on the one hand, an electorally successful organisation and, on the other, an open party that empowers citizens. The change we need is not merely a means to achieve electoral victory (although, as the chapters in this volume show, it is increasingly important to having a successful political strategy). It is also an end in itself, playing a critical role in creating a vibrant space for civic participation and deliberation. To achieve this, we believe that the Labour Party needs to:

- remove all barriers to participation;

- enable channels for dissent and debate;

- give supporters the tools to self-organise;

- keep supporters better informed; and

- reward hard work and entrepreneurialism.

Successful political parties are vital to achieving a healthy civil society, a goal shared by progressives, socialists and social democrats of all shades. Yet to continue to play this role in the 21st century, parties must transform the role of their members and supporters, turning them from clients to partners through institutions that are both empowering and relevant to the way people live their lives. The American election showed the way for genuine movement-based democratic change. It is now Britain and Labour's turn to emulate that extraordinary success.

Structure

The book is structured as follows. Each chapter details a specific aspect of the 2008 election campaign and begins with a short abstract, written by the editors, which summarises the relevant lessons for the Labour Party. Chapters 2 and 3 offer broad narratives of the election. Robert Shapiro of Columbia University sets events in the context of national divisions created by the Bush presidency. Kate Kenski from the University of Arizona then examines the historic role played by women in 2008, both as candidates and voters.

The next three chapters by David Lammy MP, grass-roots activist Ben Brandzel, and two Labour Party members who volunteered for Obama – Karin Christiansen and Marcus Roberts – examine the techniques that Barack Obama used to mobilise his supporters and volunteers.

Chapters 7 to 10 detail some of the technological developments in the election. Jennifer Stromer-Galley of the University at Albany, SUNY looks at the impact of web 2.0; Faiz Shakir of ThinkProgress.org writes about the role of the blogoshere; Matthew McGregor discusses fundraising; and Yair Ghitza and Todd Rogers – two progressive political analysts – consider the importance of statistical techniques such as microtargeting and randomised controlled experiments. In chapter 11, newly elected US Representative Glenn Nye provides a unique personal story about his successful congressional race in Virginia against an incumbent Republican.

The editors then offer a broader conclusion, examining what the 2008 election means for the future of political organising in general and for the Labour Party in particular.

The excitement, enthusiasm and hope generated by the 2008 election stands in stark contrast to the previous eight years of American history. George W Bush's presidency started under the cloud created by the 'hanging chads' controversy in Florida in 2000, and then encompassed the tragic events of 9/11, the divisiveness of two foreign wars, the polarising 2004 election, Hurricane Katrina and, finally, economic meltdown.

In this chapter, Robert Shapiro examines how the 2008 election relates to the hugely divisive Bush years, and finds that while certain events – notably the nomination of Sarah Palin as John McCain's running mate – did reanimate long-standing partisan divisions, the ultimate victor in the election cycle was enthusiasm for the democratic process.

The UK, where our faith in politics seems to be in terminal decline, could learn much from this. In particular, it seems that civil society contains the seeds of its own regeneration. Given the opportunity, and a belief that they can have a meaningful impact, citizens will re-engage and be re-enthused. The challenge for British politicians is to create an environment where this can happen.

2. Retrospective on the election: divisiveness and democracy
Robert Y Shapiro

The 2008 American election campaign that began in early 2007 was arguably the most exciting and important one since Franklin D Roosevelt's victory in 1932. The United States was engaged, with no end in sight, in wars in Iraq and Afghanistan; the country's economy was stagnant or on the downswing; and the electorate was dissatisfied with eight years of the Republican presidential administration, as reflected in President George W Bush's low and declining approval rating in the polls.

The highly ideological and partisan conflict over economic and social issues that had increased steadily since the 1970s had heightened over foreign policy and war issues leading into the 2008 election campaign.[1] President Bush continued to be the 'great divider' not 'uniter' that he had promised to be, and both John McCain and Barack Obama, as they became their parties' candidates, once again promised to end partisan conflict. Both could credibly claim that they were not extremists in their parties, and this kept New York City Mayor Michael Bloomberg from running as a third-party candidate to capture any wide open political centre.

The nation waited for the campaigns to unfold – and for any surprises. It was a good bet that like the 2000 and 2004 elections the outcome would hinge on whether Obama could win the politically close states of Ohio and Florida. All signs were that he could, because in close elections the campaign matters and Obama would take his strong campaign organisation from the primaries and out-campaign McCain in the general election, focusing on the nation's dissatisfaction with the failures of Bush's Republican administration.

In addition to the question of continued partisan divisiveness, the 2008 election posed fundamental challenges for American democracy.[2] For one, there were questions about the right to vote and whether votes would be counted accurately. The 2000 election results had been contested and ultimately decided by the Unites States Supreme Court in a partisan fashion, and in 2004 there were widespread claims of procedural irregularities, broken or defective voting machines, eligible voters not permitted to vote, and long lines that discouraged voters from casting ballots.

There were also other major questions about equality and democracy: Would racism in America prevent Barack Obama from being the nation's first African American president? Would opinion polls prove to be inaccurate in ways that undermined any positive role that polling can have to enhance American democracy?[2] Would money – campaign contributions – dominate the electoral process and continue existing political inequalities?

How, then, did democracy and divisiveness fare in the election? In short, election day 2008 was a good day for American democracy: Foremost, the US elected its first African American president, overcoming the seeming rock-solid racial barrier established at the nation's founding with its legacy of slavery. While the election of Republican Sarah Palin as the first women vice president would have been a major achievement, the racial breakthrough for the presidency was a monumental result.

Second, despite widespread concerns that led to very careful election monitoring around the country, there were, overall, no significant problems encountered in the voting process and in tallying votes. There was no evidence of vote fraud, in the wake of fears and accusations made by Republicans during the campaign. There were long lines in some places on election day, and also when 'early voting' occurred in many states, but voters waited patiently for the most part. Extraordinarily telling was that voters waited in very long queues in places such as New York City, where there was no doubt that Obama would win their state and where there were virtually no competitive elections on the ballot. While voter turnout nationally among all segments of the electorate was not as large as expected (very likely because the election was not going to be close in many states), it surpassed the turnout in the very close 2000 and 2004 elections and was estimated to be 61.6 per cent of the voting eligible population.[3]

What about the polls? The pre-election polls were extraordinarily accurate nationally and in the key states that enabled Obama to win the Electoral Vote by a large margin.[4] The public itself had followed the many and widely publicised polls right up to election day. Daily reports on cable television and on major web sites – especially realclearpolitics.com, fivethirtyeight.com, and pollster.com – proved particularly popular. This accuracy refuted decisively the great suspicion before the election that white voters would tell pollsters they would vote for the black candidate Obama, when in fact they would not.

This polling error might occur through what was called the 'Bradley Effect,' named after a black candidate for Governor of California in the 1980s about whom whites allegedly lied in opinion polls; or it might happen because many Republican voters or other McCain supporters did not respond to polls, and this could not be corrected by 'weighting' the data.

A different concern was that the pre-election polling done by telephone would be inaccurate because it failed to reach voters who only used a mobile phone. This did not materialise either. The exit polls themselves avoided this difficulty by requiring weighting to offset a bias toward the Democratic candidate. The unadjusted exit poll results which overestimated the Democrat Obama's support, however, were not leaked early so that the confusion caused by the exit polls in 2000 and 2004 was avoided.[5] The major television networks were cautious in not projecting the winner in any state until all the polls in that state had closed. In closely contested states they even waited for enough votes to be counted to ensure their projections were correct.

And the influence of money in politics? On this the 2008 election raised more questions than it answered. On the one hand, the Democrats could claim that Obama raised money from record numbers of people who gave small amounts, just as he also attracted large numbers of activists to work on his campaign, again showing the vibrancy of American democracy in the 2008 election.

At the same time, however, Obama 'flip flopped' on his original promise to take the fixed amount of federal money for his presidential election campaign and forego other contributions. In contrast, McCain took the federal funds, agreeing not to raise other cash. Obama's campaign broke all past fundraising and spending records, which included large number of donors who gave the maximum $4,600 contribution to the presidential candidate (not counting the large contributions to both political parties that were spent on the election).

Thus it is difficult to claim the election, despite the bipartisan efforts at campaign finance reform led by McCain, produced any positive change from the past with respect to the potential influence of large donors or of those who could pool together – or 'bundle' – the maximum contributions from many donors.[6] While the large number of small dollar donors was democratizing in that it brought many more people more fully into the process of political participation, the extent to which this will diminish the influence of large donors is an open question.

Last, did the campaign end partisan divisiveness and heat? It did not and if anything, it kept temperature levels high. At least two things prevented the end of partisan bickering. First, McCain's selection of Sarah Palin as his vice presidential running mate appealed to the conservative base of the Republican Party, which increased the visibility of the ideological differences between the parties.

Second, the financial crisis made the economy the dominant issue. The economy suddenly and dramatically overshadowed all of the other election issues combined – the Iraq war, terrorism, health care, and energy – as the financial crisis raised the spectre of a recession on the scale of the Great Depression. The urgent need for the government action magnified the differences between Democrats and Republicans regarding government regulation and intervention, in which the Republicans could be portrayed as falling short during the past eight years.

In the end, the 2008 election was as divisive in partisan terms as 2004, but there were two differences that not only affected the election outcome but also have major implications for the future of American politics and partisanship.[7] First, the percentage of self-identified Democrat and Republican voters was evenly divided at 37 per cent in 2004, whereas Democrats outnumbered Republicans 39 to 32 per cent in 2008. Americans clearly rejected the Republican brand name after electing Bush for his second term.

This resulted not only in Obama's election but also in larger Democratic majorities in Congress. Second, the economic failure that ensured a decisive victory for the Democrats has provided an issue for which they are now responsible and will be judged depending on whether they can lead the United States to economic recovery. Both whether and how the Democrats succeed in this mission will have long term consequences. If they succeed fully, they are likely to regain the dominance they had from the 1933 to 1968, during which time Dwight Eisenhower was the only Republican president. In the process they may also lessen partisan tension.

If, however, Obama and the Democrats succeed only by governing through sheer force of party numbers in Congress (which would have been easier if they had a majority caucus of 60 in the Senate), then it will take a decisive result in dealing with a dire national problem to lower the temperature level of partisan conflict. But if President Obama's economic policies fall short, the parties will remain evenly matched.

In such circumstances, Obama can only hope to be a 'uniter' and not a 'divider' if he genuinely attempts to take action through bipartisan efforts and leadership of the sort that both he and McCain had promised in their campaigns.

While the 2008 US election did not smash the glass ceiling in the end, it did, as Hillary Clinton memorably said, put eighteen million cracks in it. With that many votes in the primary season, Clinton came closer than any women candidate to winning the presidential nomination of a major party. Her near miss was followed by Sarah Palin's nomination as the Republican Party's first ever female candidate for vice president. These two historic events fundamentally altered public perception of America's readiness for a female president.

In this chapter Kate Kenski analyses voter and media reaction to these two female candidates and the role of women voters. These observations hold important lessons for the UK too. While progress towards equality has been made throughout the West, there are many hurdles still facing women seeking high office. In particular, there is a tendency by the media to interpret the actions of female candidates through the prism of their gender, often in a way that harms their chances of winning.

On the other hand, female voters can play a decisive role in the outcome of an election. Obama's positive message appealed to women who preferred him to McCain by 13 percentage points. This contrasts with recent British history. According to British Election Study data, the Conservatives have performed disproportionately well among female voters in every election since 1964, bar one. Labour must consider this in building its coalition for the next election and beyond.

3. Gender and the election
Kate Kenski

Women have been seeking the presidency since Victoria Woodhull ran in 1872. However, they have often not been treated by the press as viable candidates in comparison to their male opponents. The 'first woman' narrative and observations about appearance are often emphasised at the expense of the candidate's issue platform. When women candidates are criticised, their detractors proclaim that it was not the gender of the candidate that was the problem in supporting her; they just did not like that particular woman. There is a long history of that particular woman not being deemed suitable for the presidency in the court of American public opinion.

With the candidacies of Senator Hillary Clinton for Democratic nominee and Governor Sarah Palin for vice president, the 2008 election campaign helped crack the glass ceiling to some extent. Clinton's candidacy came closest to date to achieving a major party nomination for a woman, but although being a woman helped her with certain demographic groups, it hurt with others as gender stereotypes remained.

The 2008 Democratic primaries and caucuses

Senator Hillary Clinton of New York was positioned as the front-runner for the Democratic nomination before the first Democratic caucuses and primaries had taken place.

Several polls had her leading Senator Barack Obama by margins of two to one. "The new AP-Yahoo! poll shows Clinton snaring 47 per cent of support nationwide, with Sen. Barack Obama a distant second," wrote Maggie Haberman of the *New York Post*.[1] To be sure, as former First Lady, Clinton initially had much higher name recognition than the Junior Senator from Illinois.

The Clinton campaign had not spent as much time in the small caucus states as did the Obama campaign. Iowa, the first state on the nomination calendar, is the thirtieth most populated state in the Union, and had only 57 delegates to the Democratic National Convention, including twelve super delegates. Given that 2,118 of 4,234 delegates were needed to secure the nomination, concentrating on states with larger delegate counts was central to the Clinton campaign strategy. Ultimately, this proved to be a cataclysmic mistake. When Clinton came in third in Iowa, having garnered 29 per cent of the vote, compared to Obama's 38 per cent and John Edward's 30 per cent, the media called into question Clinton's viability, contending that she was no longer ahead in the horse race.[2]

Obama's rise in the polls was likely influenced in part by the news media that framed stories about him positively during the most critical part of the primary season when people were just beginning to pay attention to the campaigns. A content analysis of media coverage between January 1 and March 9 conducted by the Pew Research Center revealed that the narratives of the media stories about Obama and Clinton were comparably positive in tone.[3] The Pew study notes, "The year 2008 started off extremely well for Obama. Positive assertions commanded 77 per cent of the narrative studied about him from January 1 – 13. By March 9, the figure had dropped to 53 per cent."[4] However, while the positive tone for Obama decreased over time, the damage had already been done in unseating Clinton as the front runner.

In the next contest, the New Hampshire primary campaign, Clinton had a press conference where she discussed the importance of the campaign to her personally. In response to an undecided voter who asked "How did you get out the door every day? I mean, as a woman, I know how hard it is to get out of the house and get ready. Who does your hair?" Clinton joked and then responded in a tone that was more emotive than her usual, direct, matter-of-fact style. "I just don't want to see us fall backward as a nation," she said. "I mean, this is very personal for me. Not just political. I see what's happening. We have to reverse it."[5]

More significant than the event itself was the media's interpretation of the event, which evoked gender stereotypes about women being 'too' emotional and weak to serve as leaders.[6] The media spin and amount of coverage given to the event underscored the double-bind that women running for public office often face. If women look too tough and detached, they are criticised for not being female or human enough. If they show emotion, their credibility as potential leaders is called into question.

Afterwards, reporters were quick to attribute Clinton's win in New Hampshire not to her experience or the strength of her candidacy but to the 'near-tear' effect. "Analysts also will long debate the effect of Clinton's show of emotion here Monday, where she choked up and held back tears as she described the rigors of a presidential race. Female candidates aren't supposed to cry because it's thought to make them look soft or weak," wrote *Newsday*'s Craig Gordon the day after the primary. "But it's just possible that a near-tear or two might have helped melt Clinton's Ice Queen image or gained her a little sympathy at least."[7]

Although the media frequently characterise women as a swing vote, it is interesting to note that white women were a much more dependable voting bloc for Clinton than were white men for either candidate. In the 38 states that had exit poll data broken down by party and gender, the results showed that white women voted for Clinton in higher proportions than they did Obama. Women were more inclined to vote for Obama over Clinton in only four states: Illinois, New Mexico, Vermont, and Oregon. Utah was a draw with both candidates receiving 49 per cent of the white female vote each. White men, however, varied greatly from state to state. In 22 of the states where exit poll data was available, white men supported Clinton over Obama. In 14 states, white men supported Obama over Clinton. In two states, white men evenly split for Clinton and Obama: Delaware and Texas.

During the campaign, the National Annenberg Election Survey (NAES), a survey of adults in the US, asked people, "If you voted today in the Democratic presidential primary election or caucus in your state, which candidate would you vote for?" Figures 1 and 2 show the trends in support for Clinton and Obama among white women and white males respectively. These figures suggest that there was slightly less stability among the vote preferences of white males than white females. If gender and race both played a part in one's vote decision, then white males were a cross-pressured group.

Unlike white voters, black voters were consistent in their vote preferences and favoured Obama by a factor of 2:1 or greater in every state except Clinton's own New York.[8] Disaggregated by gender, the data suggests that black females did not feel as cross-pressured as did white males. Nonetheless, most voters said that neither gender nor race were important factors in their vote decisions.

Among those who reported that either gender or race was an important factor in their vote decisions, the declaration did not necessarily mean that it was used negatively against the candidates. In some instances, being female appeared to have helped Clinton, and being black appeared to have helped Obama. For example, in Alabama, of those voters who said that race was an

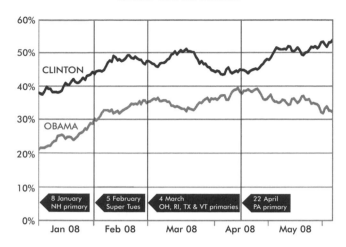

Figure 1 Vote preferences of white <u>women</u> who were Democrats or Independents across time (15-day prior moving average)[9]

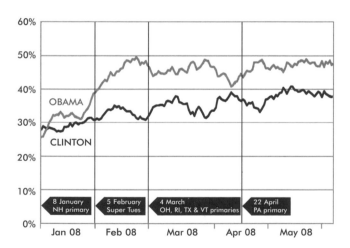

Figure 2 Vote preferences of white <u>men</u> who were Democrats or Independents across time (15-day prior moving average)[10]

important factor in deciding their vote, 62 per cent supported Obama and 35 per cent voted for Clinton; among those who said it was not important, 53 per cent voted for Obama and 45 per cent voted for Clinton. In Massachusetts, of the 20 per cent who said that gender was important in deciding their vote, 76 per cent voted for Clinton and 19 per cent voted for Obama; of those who said it was not important, 51 per cent voted for Clinton and 47 per cent voted for Obama. Yet, in some places, these factors may have worked against the candidates. In Kentucky, of those who said that race was an important factor, 81 per cent voted for Clinton and 16 per cent voted for Obama; of those who said it was not important, 61 per cent voted for Clinton and 35 per cent voted for Obama.[11]

The 2008 presidential general election

Questions about gender and its role in the outcome of the general election were brought to the fore on August 29 with the selection of Governor Sarah Palin as Senator John McCain's running mate. She was the first woman to run on a Republican presidential ticket. People wondered whether women who supported Hillary Clinton would break from their party to put a woman near the White House if not directly in it. Ultimately, Clinton voters returned to their home party by the end of the election. Exit poll voters (including Republicans and Independents) were asked "Who did you want to win the Democratic nomination?" Of the 14 per cent who said Clinton, 83 per cent ended up voting for Obama to 16 per cent for McCain.[12]

When it came to gender and the presidential vote, there was a gender gap with women preferring Obama to McCain by 13 per cent. Men gave a one per cent edge to McCain. Demonstrating the importance of disaggregating the data by race and gender, Table 1 shows that there was a sizeable gap in support between McCain and Obama among white men – a gap of 16 per cent. While not as large as that of white men, white women gave more support to McCain than Obama (53 per cent to 46 per cent). Blacks, both male and female, gave overwhelming support to Obama at a rate of 19 to one.

In previous elections, it has been assumed that the vice presidential picks did not make much of a difference in election outcomes. A presidential campaign usually hopes that the VP nominee will contribute to winning the electoral votes in his or her home state. The Palin selection, however, influenced campaign dynamics by Palin receiving an unusual amount of news coverage for a vice presidential candidate. In a content analysis of media stories aired or printed between September 8 through October 16, 2008, the Pew Research Center found that "stories that focused in one way or another on Governor Palin's impact on the race made up the No. 3 campaign topic during

Category	% of Total Vote	Obama (%)	McCain (%)	Other/No Answer (%)
Total vote	100	53	46	1
Men	47	49	48	3
Women	53	56	43	1
White men	36	41	57	2
White women	39	46	53	1
Black men	5	95	5	NA
Black women	7	96	2	NA

Table 1 The presidential vote by race and gender (%)[13]

these weeks, from explorations of her record, voter reaction to her, to her various interviews. Together, these Palin-related topics accounted for 14 per cent" of the media coverage analysed.[14]

Palin was a major component in half as many stories as Obama and McCain. She "was a significant factor" in "28 per cent of all of the election stories. That, however, is about three times that of Democratic vice presidential nominee Joe Biden (9 per cent)."[15] Perhaps most problematic for the Republican ticket was that 39 per cent of stories about Palin were negative in tone. About a third (33 per cent) of stories had a neutral or mixed tone, and 28 per cent were positive. In comparison, 33 per cent of stories about Senator Biden were positive; 53 per cent were neutral and 15 per cent were negative in the week of September 29 to October 5, which was the week in which Biden received the most coverage and was the week of the vice presidential debate.[16] In other weeks, Biden was given very little coverage, but the coverage he did

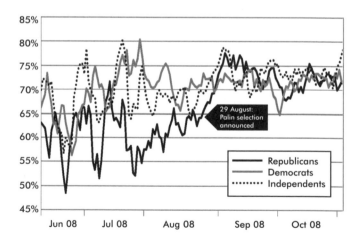

Figure 3 "Do you think the United States is ready to elect a president who is a woman, or not?" (5-day prior moving average)[17]

receive was 48 per cent negative, 35 per cent mixed, and 17 per cent positive.[18]

It is probable that the extensive negative coverage had an impact on perceptions about the little known governor from Alaska. Exit poll participants were asked if Biden and Palin were qualified to be president if necessary. While 66 per cent said that Biden was qualified, only 38 per cent said that Palin was qualified.[19] When asked if McCain's choice of Palin was a factor in their vote, 60 per cent said yes, 33 per cent said no. Of those who said yes, however, 56 per cent voted for McCain and 43 per cent voted for Obama. Of those who said no, 65 per cent voted for Obama and 33 per cent voted for McCain.[20]

Conclusion

Despite the 2008 presidential election ending without a woman president or a woman within a heartbeat of the presidency, the candidacies of Clinton for her party's nomination and Palin as the GOP vice presidential candidate changed American's perceptions of whether the country was ready for a woman president. As Clinton came within reach of receiving the Democratic nomination, perceptions on the 'woman president' question changed. Even with the negative news coverage that Palin received, her nomination helped facilitate changes in Republicans' perceptions that the US was ready for a woman president (see Figure 3). This was an important contribution to cracking the glass ceiling as Republicans and conservatives have generally been less likely to report that they would be likely to vote for a woman candidate if their party nominated one in comparison to Democrats and liberals.[21] Consequently, the 2008 presidential election deeply fractured, although did not break, the veneer of stereotypes about gender and leadership and was thus a transformative one.

In this chapter, David Lammy examines how Barack Obama built and disseminated his message. While his campaign offers a great example of successful micro-level political organisation, it also used messages that drew heavily on big ideas and themes, which were understandable and attractive to tens of millions of Americans.

Lammy draws three lessons. First, Obama's message of 'hope' and 'change' was positive and purposeful. Second, Obama's own story became synonymous with the kind of change he sought. He outlined how far the Bush administration and Republicans had drifted from the founding principles of the constitution but reassured voters that just as he was a personal embodiment of the American Dream, so too could he return the country to a rightful path. Third, Obama's message had both consistency and clarity, unlike that of either Hillary Clinton or John McCain.

In the UK, a positive message and vision of the good society, drawing both on past Labour achievements and hopes for the future, must now be wedded to the Party's administrative competence and technocratic skills. Here, Labour has a powerful story to tell. From its foundation as a movement fighting for workers' representation, to the Party that created the NHS and bought equality into the political mainstream, the Party needs to find and articulate its place in the broader progressive tradition. Crucially, this must define what Labour is for rather than what it is against and use the past as inspiration to construct a movement for the future.

4. The power of storytelling
David Lammy MP

If Barack Obama's campaign proves anything, it is that people can still be inspired by politics and the possibility of change for the better. The Illinois Senator managed to remind millions of Americans of what Martin Luther King called "the fierce urgency of now", and turned their passion into a valuable tool for his campaign. Given that we live in a time when cynicism is assumed and disengagement the dominant theme of many elections, this was no small achievement.

We need to be careful, however, in the lessons we draw from this. Even for those following the US election closely, it might have seemed that the incredible sequence of events leading up to November 2008 was the product of the interrelationship between a number of conditional circumstances – the unpopularity of the Bush administration, the growing problems in the American economy, the history-making nature of Obama's candidature, the Senator's particular gifts as an orator, and the rising potency of internet campaigning being chief among them. All these factors were certainly important. But to treat them in isolation is to misunderstand one of the major skills in modern political communication.

An important element of Obama's success came from the ability of his campaign to interweave these various elemental factors into a bigger, much broader message. Politicians and journalists frequently understand this skill as the construction of 'narrative'. Perhaps this term is slightly tarnished, seeming like a piece of 'newspeak' employed by the professional political classes. In the UK, it is certainly an expression used very frequently, often pejoratively and rather glibly. But, as Obama proved, big themes and messages are an important part of engaging people and proving that politics can be connected with their lives – and is the glue that can hold a movement together. But this leaves one big question, vital for anyone trying to establish what happened in 2008 and understand the lessons that progressives in other countries can learn: just how was this achieved?

Generation change

If the Obama team had one important message for Americans, it was that what they were doing was not about politics as usual. When she launched her campaign, Hillary Clinton forcefully said that she was "in it to win it". Compare this with Obama's opening salvo of the campaign, when he declared that "I want to win the next battle... for justice and opportunity... for better schools, and better jobs, and health care for all... I'm in this race – not just to hold an office, but to gather with you to transform a nation."[1] This difference of emphasis highlights something very fundamental about the Obama message and what they were trying to achieve. They were not just in the business of winning, but winning for the purpose of changing the world.

This fits with the themes that most people associate with the Obama campaign, the twin mantras of hope and change. These ideas certainly were important, but a few observations need to be made about exactly how they were used. Obama's claim to represent change was partly about age, and partly about politics. Although they might not admit it today, senior figures in the Obama campaign knew there was a generational divide in the US. For many younger Americans, there was a huge desire to move beyond conflicts that had defined the country for the past four decades, from the Johnson and Nixon administrations to the 'culture wars' over abortion, gay rights and gun control during the Bush years. By 2008, millions of citizens were uninterested in fighting yesterday's battles and frustrated by partisanship bickering in Washington. Instead they were looking for a candidate who could lead them into the future. Obama's attempt to speak to these voters was long in gestation. As early as his convention speech in 2004, he was arguing that "There's not a liberal America and a conservative America – there's the United States of America."[2]

The power of this message was accentuated because Obama's main Democratic opponent in the primary season was Hillary Clinton, one of the defining figures of the boomer generation. Clinton had another significant drawback for an electorate disappointed with recent American history. She was an insider, an expert at playing the old Washington game. This allowed the Obama team to portray her as part of the problem, while he could be the solution. This was a powerful political message.

Inheriting the progressive legacy

This rejection of 'old-style' politics and the focus on change might suggest that the Obama campaign message fetishised the new. But the point should not be oversimplified. Obama's young team had a genuine reverence for the history and achievements of reformist politics in the United States. From the moment he declared his candidacy, Obama drew on his own story as a mixed heritage American, who had earned his Senate seat through hard work on the difficult Southside of Chicago. In doing this, he came to embody the history of the American progressive struggle, and the American dream. As such, in Obama's own words, his campaign was 'the *next* great chapter in the American story'. But this wasn't just about having a candidate with a good story. His speeches explicitly linked his supporters to the abolitionists and slaves, immigrants and the Suffragist movement. His focus on his supporters and the movement he was building also rekindled the old progressive tradition of activist-focused politics and the rejection of political elites. By implication, of course, this also tied him to Lincoln, Franklin D Roosevelt, the Kennedys and King.

Obama was also able to tap into the broader heritage of the United States and effectively link his campaign to the founding principles of the Republic. The day after Obama's election as President, the *Washington Post* declared that the USA had produced "inspiring and overdue proof that the American dream was still alive."[3] The *New York Times* thought that Obama had reaffirmed "that America is the land of extraordinary opportunity."[4] The importance of such sentiments should not be underestimated. In recent decades, after all, progressives have frequently been branded as unpatriotic or somehow 'less American' than conservatives. Obama managed to reclaim the progressive element of the American tradition, which had long been defined by the Democrat's opponents, and link it to the future aspirations of millions of American families. This achievement was a vital element in the creation of a movement which inspired and mobilised millions of Americans.

The mechanics of message

The Obama message was therefore a hybrid of the old and the new. Dissemination, however, was as important as content. Three things can be said about this. First, Obama moved away from dry, technocratic and policy-heavy explanations of 'what works' (of the sort that have become fashionable among social democrats around the world in recent decades), and instead offered a far broader discussion of values and ideals – in other words, the candidate spent a lot of his time talking about 'what matters, and why'. This didn't mean that the mechanics of achieving this vision were neglected, but instead it flowed very naturally from a wider idea of the good society. This is why Obama's rhetoric was so engaging – and authentic.

Second, the message was highly focused and consistent over the length of the campaign. The themes Obama talked about remained very similar from the announcement of his candidature until his victory. During the primaries, this compared favourably with Clinton's frequent shifts and relaunches, from an original focus on experience, to trying to claim the 'change' mantle, and finally attempting to become the voice of blue collar Democrats. During the presidential election, the Obama team kept the same themes but turned their message on the Republicans – successfully making the point that only a Democratic victory could offer a decisive break with the Bush era. This was a significant accomplishment, given the 'maverick' reputation of John McCain. Furthermore, the Obama team never allowed itself to be deflected by increasingly desperate attacks by the right over the course of the campaign.

Third, the message was expressed with clarity, sometimes being reduced to single words or slogans (such as hope, change and 'yes we can'). This approach to communication has a number of advantages: as well as making it easier to retain focus over the length of the campaign, it provided very effective branding. It gave supporters simple ideas to latch onto and use on the doorstep, and fitted neatly into the desire of the rolling news channels to play succinct clips in their reports. There are dangers though. This kind of politics can lead to accusations that a campaign is somehow intellectually lightweight and content-free. It is hard to level this accusation at Obama, however. Although key messages were kept short, these were distillations of much more complex ideas and beliefs, which were available on his web site, in his books and in speeches, such as the More Perfect Union address on race. As a result, there was a direct link between short slogans and big ideas.

Conclusion

We should not write off the achievements of the centre-left in the 1990s, on either side of the Atlantic. At the time, the left urgently needed to start to redress the great injustices and inequalities created by right wing governments in the eighties, as well as rehabilitate its own reputation after the end of the Cold War. In doing so, New Labour achieved its success less by outlining its own vision of the good society and more by defining what it was against: the poor quality of public services and inequality created by the Conservative government on the one hand and hard-left intransigence on the other. This strategy was both successful and necessary, but ultimately it was very defensive. The 2008 American election indicates that this period in the history of the left is coming to an end. The Obama campaign did not exist in the intellectual space created by its opponents, and instead was fundamentally about changing America. Furthermore, because it was not so defensive, the Obama campaign was able to fight much harder to link the broader progressive tradition to long held American values. Since the seventies, American conservatives had been hugely successful at portraying reformist ideas as being the antithesis of the interests and principles of ordinary Americans. Obama's narrative of American history contested this argument in the most vigorous way for a generation.

This is not just a matter of electoral expediency though. The political environment which created both the New Democrats and New Labour is rapidly dissipating, as the financial crisis dismantles longstanding certainties. On both sides of the Atlantic then, now is a time for political vision and a discussion of what the world should look like in the future. As Obama did, politicians need to shift their focus from the immediate and short-term, and instead ask what kind of institutions and systems we want to bequeath our children. At this time it is vitally important that progressives and social democrats all over the world clearly articulate their values, as only parties that believe in collectivism are in a position to recognise and act on the limits of the market. And only collectivism gives us the opportunity to put society first, whether that means reforming financial markets and the banking sector, preventing young people from being targeted by advertising, allowing families to spend more time with each other, or stopping new betting shops being set up in communities already well-served by bookmakers. The state is there to help society govern the market – not to stand back and hope for the best, as the right would like to do. These were the values embedded in Obama's campaign – and are at the heart of the modern Labour Party, too.

In this chapter, Ben Brandzel explains how Barack Obama did not create the movement that elected him. Rather, it created him. The mobilisation of progressives online – begun by MoveOn in the late 1990s and then employed by Howard Dean during his unsuccessful bid for the Democratic nomination in 2004 – was perfected rather than produced by the Obama campaign.

In several important respects, Britain is even better placed than American to foster genuine movement-based politics, argues Brandzel. However, while there is an appetite for change, and although our parliamentary system has the advantage that power sits with parties rather than individual politicians, British political culture and our parties, with their fee-paying models of membership, remain behind the curve.

Brandzel explains that online mass movements provide a new form of discourse where organisations are pulled towards the common sense centre. He urges Britons dissatisfied with their democracy to stop vicariously following developments across the pond and start their own movement.

5. A British movement for change
Ben Brandzel

On January 21st 2009, almost every major newspaper in the world dedicated their front page to pictures of Barack Obama's inauguration as the 44th President of the United States. This was the culmination of an improbable and exhilarating story that captivated the world for the better part of two years.

Why was the world so enraptured with this American election in which they could play no direct role? In part, it was because consequences of the Bush Presidency, which were a painful reality to so many around the world, including in the United Kingdom, had clearly illuminated the direct relationship between American decisions and global impact. In part too, it was because Obama's stirring rhetoric and luminous vision touched the hearts of all who heard it, as would any work of inspirational theatre or prose. But there was also something more, which holds the real lesson of the US election for the UK.

Obama's victory was improbable not just because of America's legacy of racism or because he had started a long way behind the Clinton juggernaut. It was improbable because his campaign relied so famously on the contributions, energy, creativity, and participation of millions to overcome his disadvantages. His victory, then, was the victory of passion over 'inevitability', of collective effort over collective inertia. It was a victory people everywhere could feel a part of, because people everywhere who long for change have a stake in that sort of struggle.

I spent several months in the UK in 2008 before I shipped back to North Carolina to work on Obama's campaign. I was struck how at some point the British press stopped bothering to contextualise US election stories as being about another country. The candidates were named and discussed in shorthand just as if they were running for Parliament – and usually given much more coverage than the latest row in Westminster. It's probably fair to say that given the 'special relationship' between our nations, no other country on earth was more hooked into this fabulous story than the UK.

Yet at the same time, I kept hearing the rueful opinion that none of this would be possible over here. The British people, I was told, were far too apathetic, far too disengaged, far too convinced that their voice – no matter how loud – would fall on the deaf ears of politicians who couldn't be bothered. Plus, as I was frequently reminded, "there is no British Obama". All of this casts a rather sad tinge to the cathartic obsession with the America election – it's as if many Brits gave up looking for vibrant democracy in their own lives and resolved to experience it vicariously in ours.

Well, in response to all of this self-depreciating civic gloom I have only one of my favourite British aphorisms: *rubbish*. Why? Because the 'there is no British Obama' claim fundamentally misunderstands what just happened in America – and is in fact fatally counter-productive to replicating it here.

Building a movement for change

It's obviously true that Obama's sensational talent as a campaigner and the outstanding accomplishments of his campaign cannot be underestimated. But they were able to succeed in a particular context, and that context was a long fought, hard won victory in and of itself.

Here's the first point to remember: only a few short years before last months' triumphant inauguration, George W Bush had stolen an election and was peddling grave falsehoods to the American people, yet was basking in the highest approval ratings of any sitting president in American history. Instead of "yes we can" we had "you're either with us or against us" and "bring it on." Critiquing the administration's foreign policy was loudly called treason. Civic duty was reduced to shopping. Global warming was officially denied. And those of us who felt differently about any of it were quite fearful that either we, or everyone else around us, had gone stark raving mad. And you know who changed all of this? It was not an obscure state legislator from Illinois. It was the people ourselves.

I was lucky enough to have a front row seat for this transformation through my work with MoveOn.org. MoveOn began as a simple plea for sanity when a modest California couple put up an online petition to oppose the impeachment of President Clinton and sent it to 60 of their friends. In a few months, half a million people had signed. It grew bigger when a young nonprofit worker and his roommate put out a simple request that America and her allies treat 9/11 as a crime and punish the guilty – not seize it as a pretext for war. He sent their petition to his friends, and within days several hundred thousand people from every state and dozens of nations had added their name. Of course, President Clinton was impeached and Iraq was invaded. But people who knew it was wrong were linked together – and so the seeds of change were sewn.

Over the next seven years, MoveOn grew to more than five million members and its volunteers organised over 130,000 local events in every corner of the country. A teacher in Boise, Idaho gathered friends from church to protest the nomination of an extreme conservative Supreme Court Chief Justice, and minds were changed. An accountant from Albany, New York went with his wife and brother to hand their Congressman letters from constituents defending the food stamp program – and a vote was switched. A librarian from Atlanta, Georgia got on the local news for her efforts to defend social security from privatisation, and a generation was saved.

What are the characteristics of this type of politics? The groups that practice it have a different organisational model to more traditional institutions. They are driven by the grassroots, and energised by the collective action of regular people. They do have a leadership, but these people are 'stewards'. As a result, those managing the organisation act on behalf of the membership, not the other way around. Crucially, while such movements exist to articulate a deeply held political worldview, they remain independent of political parties, and are willing to express the views of their members to both friends and opponents.

The power of this model of organizing was illustrated by the electoral potency of our movement. The Bush era did not end in 2008. It ended in 2006, when voters delivered his party in Congress the greatest rout in a generation. There was no single Barack Obama to anchor or inspire that campaign, but MoveOn members used online tools to make seven million phone calls to swing congressional districts driving key voters to the polls.

Of course, MoveOn and all its work is in fact just one very small piece in a very large puzzle. During this same time span the Howard Dean campaign in 2004 revolutionised presidential politics when ordinary people funded and rallied around a cry for change – even when that cry came from a less gifted but thoroughly sincere politician who I don't think ever really imagined himself president. There have been several other major online movement organisations very like MoveOn, and countless other organisations of every shape and size operating at a local, state and national level whose members played a vital role in moving the country towards that moment we all witnessed on January 20th.

And to be clear, none of this background in any way diminishes the obvious skill and magnetic power of Obama as a candidate, or the stupendous organizing feat of the Obama campaign. But Obama himself is quite aware of his context. I was sitting in the stadium that starry night in Denver when Obama looked up and told 75,000 people, "this campaign has never been about me. It's about you." That oft repeated line wasn't just rhetoric, and he wasn't only talking about his election supporters. He was talking about everything a nation of stubborn believers did to pave the way.

So if you want to find the next Obama movement, don't wait for the next Obama – start the next movement. And the good news is, there's reason to believe that here in UK the next movement is already well underway.

Exporting movement politics? Yes we can.

No matter how complacent, disengaged or conservative you think the British population may look today, I promise it doesn't look any more so than the nation of shopping, war-mongering cowboys America was made out to be just a short while ago. I believe the hunger for people-powered-change is quite evident across your nation. But tapping into it may require challenging a lot of assumptions about the way things are done.

Last May, I was talking with a Labour Party official involved in the London Mayoral campaign about how they might make the most of Obama's online tools. They had one tool, for example, that allowed volunteers to host house meetings, make the case for Ken, self-organise volunteer squads, and decentralise the entire campaign in an exciting new way. But they essentially weren't using it. I asked why not, and was told it was because British people, unlike Americans, just wouldn't feel comfortable meeting in their living rooms with friends and strangers to talk about their lives and politics. "Really? "I asked. "Even in London?" "Yes." He assured me, "It's just not British."

That same evening, I went to an 'accountability session' organised by a local community organizing outfit called London Citizens. All the mayoral candidates were there, but there were no stump speeches or standard pleas for support. Rather, the meeting revolved around the group's five-point agenda for improving life in London. All the candidates had to give clear yes or no answers about whether they would implement it. I had never seen such a raw display of people power in an electoral setting. And where did the agenda come from? It was synthesised from 1,200 house meetings organised over several months by London Citizens. At each party, Londoners gathered in their living rooms with friends and strangers to discuss their lives and politics – precisely what I had just been told couldn't be done.

The British people, it seems to me, are already a bit ahead of the curve. It's no accident that Obama's 2008 campaign strategy emerged from his background as a community organiser. And Britain's political apparatus would do well to look to Britain's organisers to discover what British citizens are ready to do – and do very well – when given the chance.

Further, for the political parties to accommodate true movement-driven change, they simply have to be more open to robust, grassroots involvement. In the internet era, the old model of dues-paying membership has become a barrier to entry and is now a bulwark against mass participation and strength. I know the Labour Party in particular has been scarred before by outside invasion – I can't go a day without hearing some horror story about the 'Bennites' or the 'Trots' – but this is a different world.

In fact, by keeping the Party apparatus closed and small, you ensure your own vulnerability. Decisions made in cramped backrooms can always be over-whelmed by a few persistent malcontents who speak louder and longer than everyone else – or powerful special interests who can buy or coerce their way to the top. Mass movements open to anyone who can log on or get together when they have a spare moment will always be pulled towards the common sense centre. It's why Wikipedia can self-police for accuracy, why Obama's open forums never seriously embarrassed the candidate and why the London Citizens' agenda called for things like ensuring the Olympic Village creates public housing – not erecting statues to Che.

What's more, if the parties did open up, I truly believe the British system is naturally better posi-tioned to foster movement-based change than the American one. Despite three decades where British elections have become increasingly 'presidentalised', you still vote for a party and its platform, and not for an individual whose personal life must embody all your hopes and dreams. Movements form around val-ues, issues, ways of seeing the world and longing for a better way of life. Individuals can certainly lead them, but for movements to be strong, single individuals cannot truly embody them. Your parliamentary democracy gives each party the chance to be about so much more than its spokespeople or officials. And your electorate is used to voting for parties whose val-ues they believe in. Structurally, it's a system ripe for movement politics – if only the institutions dominat-ing that system would stop getting in the way. To adapt another Obama aphorism, it could also be argued that change doesn't come *from* Westminster, change comes *to* Westminster. British civil society is replete with NGOs campaigning for a better way of life, and new ones are popping up all the time.

One particularly promising group I've helped get going is called 38 Degrees (www.38Degrees.org.uk), set to launch this spring. It's inspired by MoveOn and its sister group, GetUp, in Australia. Using the full power of online and offline organizing techniques, their aim is to harness the rising tide of progressive frustration and aspiration to unite a large, nimble, grassroots force for change on a whole range of pressing issues. In nature, 38 degrees is the tipping point angle at which an avalanche begins. This new effort, and the many other related initiatives emerging throughout British society, should provide hope to even the deepest cynic that an avalanche of change may not be far away.

I know this vision of anonymous, issue driven leadership seems quite counter-intuitive when our picture of movement politics is so dominated by its recent culmination in the very personality driven Obama campaign. But that's why the movement history that paved the way is so vital to understand – and why seeking the 'British Obama' in the form of a singular, charismatic equivalent is not only unnecessary, but fatally counter-productive to what must happen here if the UK is to successfully follow suit.

Conclusion

A little competitive give-and-take in the race towards progress is nothing new for our societies. The British brought democracy into the modern world. Then our Founding Fathers fought a revolution because those rights didn't extend far enough across the Atlantic. Then you abolished slavery and the slave trade. Then we enfranchised American women on equal terms to men. Then you established universal health care. Now we've spawned a movement that elected Barack Obama. I believe the British answer is not nearly as far off as you might think. And when it comes, it's going to be great. Watch out for the avalanche!

Obama's campaign adopted the motto 'respect, empower, and include' to describe their volunteer operation. Far from being a set of buzzwords, Karin Christiansen and Marcus Roberts argue that this slogan summed up the values of the entire movement. Using a combination of trust and technology, the Obama campaign ensured that volunteers were valued, authorised to manage their own time and make their own local decisions, and judged on their merits and overall contribution.

Obama mixed the old with the new. The campaign's effort to recruit, train and motivate its activists was unlike anything seen in previous election cycles, as was the autonomy enjoyed by supporters. But the vertical organisational structure and the tasks that volunteers were asked to undertake – door-knocking, phone banking, and leafleting – was identical to other campaigns.

Christiansen and Roberts argue that although the Labour Party will not emulate Obama's army of supporters any time soon, they can learn from the way he treated them. Ideas such as recruiting volunteers beyond the Party's membership and spending more time training and motivating are recommended. Nonetheless, these reforms will fall flat if Labour does not undergo a more fundamental cultural change away from managing meetings and towards delivering campaigns.

6. 'Respect, empower and include': the new model army

Karin Christiansen and Marcus Roberts

The Obama campaign represented a revolution in political volunteering, and proved just how potent direct-contact politics – long regarded as the poor relation to 'air-war' style, media-based campaigning – could be. The sheer scale of what was achieved was staggering. In early September, for example, Obama supporters were able to call as many voters in Ohio in a single night as the Republicans had planned to contact during the entire month. These achievements were replicated across all the battleground states and throughout the election.

It would be easy to misunderstand what was achieved. This was not just about numbers, and nor was the volunteer organisation constructed only around the candidate, formidable though Barack Obama proved to be. More important was the organisational ideology that created the largest grassroots political action in American history.

At the heart of all of this was the campaign's slogan of 'Respect, empower and include'. Respect was the idea that a positive and professional culture was the most important component in building real trust between staff and volunteers. This empowered volunteers to make local decisions about the use of time and resources without constantly consulting up the chain of command. Technological innovations helped achieve this goal, by allowing individuals to organise canvassing or phone-banking on their own timetable through my.barackobama.com. This open approach meant the campaign was able to include both longstanding veterans and political first timers, improving both the scale and efficiency of the operation, and, as importantly, creating a positive collective feeling of professional commitment and personal ownership.

As survivors of both Labour and Democratic Party campaigns, we were struck by the extent to which respecting, empowering and including people was more than just a slogan for chatter with reporters or pretty posters on office walls. These words were also core values of the campaign. At a minimum they helped mitigate the usual tensions and frictions of campaign life while at best they inspired volunteers to do that extra canvass round, ask friends and families to join them, and even make those small donations that funded the campaign juggernaut. 'Respect, empower and include' manifested itself in five specific elements of volunteer management which we discuss in turn below: recruitment, structure, training, motivation, and monitoring.

'Respect, empower, and include' in practice

Volunteers were recruited through party, union and political action committee lists; at set piece events, ranging from massive rallies to small-scale house parties; and using both traditional and new media advertising. My.BarackObama.com was central to this, enabling volunteers to self-organise, and allowing campaign staff to coordinate groups and make connections based on a volunteer's locality or interests. They could also use online tools to contact their personal networks of friends, family and neighbours, and tell them about what they were doing and ask if they wanted to be involved. The range of different approaches meant that half the volunteers were participating in their first political campaign. As a result, a large recruitment structure grew organically from the ground up but was directed and fed from the top down. Indeed, this combination of grassroots control, and the centre's ability to exercise meaningful command where necessary, was a key condition of Obama's success. It meant, for example, that the prioritisation of volunteer recruitment and training during the summer months could be sustained when many activists were desperate to move on to voter contact. This is not to say that the level of devolution was tension-free or that the balance was always correct, but the decentralisation of operational control meant that the campaign got it right more often than not.

Once volunteers were recruited, the campaign went out of its way to create a wide array of opportunities for different forms of activism. While the essence of the campaign volunteer operation lay in the hard-nosed business of knocks and calls (canvassing and phone banking), volunteers could also be slotted into other positions. Runners got canvassing packs from headquarters to those in the field, 'visibility events' involved volunteers waving signs at important intersections on election days, and 'comfort captains' provided the troops with everything from home made lasagne to tray after tray of Dunkin' Donuts for those returning from the front line. Volunteers smoothly slotted into the organisation in line with their talents and desire to be involved.

But within the array of activities lay a traditional organogram with a vertical power structure. Regional Field Directors (roughly 30 in number in a state the size of Ohio) managed scores of Field Organisers, who in turn managed roughly ten Neighbourhood Team Leaders, each responsible for coordinators of various tasks such as canvassing and phone banking, and veteran and faith groups. The primary elections taught the campaign that the most effective ratio from one tier to the next was no more than one to ten.

Key to the effectiveness of this structure was the successful training of volunteers and identification of people suitable for management positions. The amount of time that was spent training was greater than had ever previously been practiced in a political campaign. The theory was simple: volunteers with sufficient training and testing would more efficiently execute campaign field operations, and recruit and train new activists. Thus there was a cascade approach to the dissemination of skills and knowledge.

'Camp Obama' weekends were one of the most high profile approaches to training. On these courses high performing volunteers were steeped in the ethos of the campaign and given technical training in voter contact software and leadership training on volunteer management. More generally, up and down the country, people – often new to the campaign themselves – were spending time with fresh recruits until they were comfortable with the processes and tasks that they were to carry out. In making decisions about management positions, campaign staff generally used observations of good performance at more junior levels or information about previous campaign experience provided by a volunteer on their MyBO profile. This meant that, on signing up to volunteer, you could quickly rise to a staff position as a Field Organiser, managing ten Neighbourhood Team leaders, each responsible for four or five co-ordinators and 40-60 volunteers.

Once volunteers had been recruited and trained, significant efforts were made to keep them motivated. This was achieved through all manner of traditional methods such as regular encouragement and thanks, clear explanations of how their efforts were contributing to the bigger picture, and ensuring that the basic equipment and tools they needed (for example, good maps and directions, spare phones to make calls) were readily available. Motivation was clearly helped by the general sense of the importance of the volunteer effort, which was aided by the willingness of the candidate and the senior staff to communicate directly with volunteers through a creative mix of fundraising and media events, conference calls, and web videos. Two days before the election, for example, the candidate himself took part in a conference call with volunteers and encouraged them by saying, "let's see how this baby runs." The election itself was, of course, the most motivating force with volunteers driven on by a potent brew of both enthusiasm for their candidate and antipathy for the status quo. This will be hard for Labour to replicate in the UK given that it is the incumbent party but what can be emulated is the sense that the volunteer system is important, that it is worth investing in, and that it will deliver.

Monitoring campaign performance

Striking the balance between trusting and checking the work of volunteers lay at the heart of the campaign's monitoring efforts. This was necessary because the Obama team's approach to success and failure was to create a balance between trusting their volunteers to use the available technology without supervision, but also stripping them of their portfolio if they did not prove themselves. The campaign allowed volunteers to access their own call lists and canvass sheets, complete them to their own timetable, and, vitally, enter their own response information. Campaigns have traditionally resisted such openness because they were fearful that it exposes the core of field operations (in particular, the metrics of response rates) to the opposition, and risks undermining the integrity of the dataset.

These were considered acceptable risks so long as there was a sufficient volume of data entered. Spot checks were important to ensure that volunteers who were entering fabricated information or exaggerating their returns were caught. It has not yet been publicly stated how much spot-checking of returns was undertaken, but it appears that particularly high-performing volunteers had their numbers verified, while low-performing assistants were left largely unchecked. So, if a Neighbourhood Team Leader came back from a 20-person canvassing operation and reported a particularly high number of doors knocked, the Field Organiser would ring a couple of numbers and begin the call by saying, "I'm from the Obama campaign. Have you been called already this evening?" If it turned out they had not, the volunteer was confronted and potentially restricted from accessing the database. It should be noted, however, that such instances were extremely rare.

Monitoring was also important in deciding whether to promote an individual to a position of greater responsibility. Field Organisers tested impressive volunteers for Neighbourhood Team Leader status by challenging them first to prove that they could organise a local event, then to run a canvass or phone-banking operation, and finally to demonstrate their willingness and aptitude at specific training sessions of new volunteers. Similar monitoring of fresh blood was employed at every level up the chain to campaign headquarters in Chicago.

Labour's challenge

Key to the campaign's ability to deliver on the 'respect, empower, and include' mantra was the introduction of effective technology and then trusting people to use it well. There were, of course, glitches along the way such as Votebuilder, the online database of citizens' voting intentions, grinding to a halt in many areas two nights before the election. But the resilience of the system was such that these stumbles became mere irritations as the teams on the ground found creative solutions to deal with the matter at hand.

Although it is highly unlikely that the Labour Party will have the number of volunteers that the Obama campaign recruited any time soon, there are key aspects of the approach we can learn from:

- remembering to ask and invite people to join us – whether as friends, volunteers or members;

- looking beyond the membership for volunteers;

- developing stronger relationships between CLPs and other organisations and activist groups that can provide pools of volunteers for specific campaign operations;

- spending much more time making sure both new volunteers and old members are comfortable with what they are being asked to do, especially if it involves technology that they have not used regularly;

- ensuring that those who come canvassing or take part in a phone bank are thanked personally and sincerely for their time, and are given a sense of where their efforts fit in and what they have achieved;

- trusting volunteers, and making much greater efforts to be friendly and respectful, and inspiring people towards further and deeper engagement;

- keeping our voter file open – as has recently been announced – even when things go wrong, which they will. Training and performance assessment process of volunteers to use the systems and enter their own data need to be rolled out systematically to reduce the chances of the system being corrupted.

All that said, the potential efficiencies and gains that can be learned from Obama's campaign will only be fully realised if Labour changes its culture. That means shifting the approach of many CLPs from managing meetings to delivering campaigns – fundraising, door knocking and making calls. The CLP structure has clear potential to emulate the vertical but decentralised network that underlay the Obama campaign machine. But a major change of approach is also required. For Labour to succeed in 2010 and beyond we need to embrace 'respect, empower and include', not just as buzzwords but as values. If we do, we have the potential to build a machine in the UK as formidable as the one that even senior Republican strategists recognised as unstoppable.

Barack Obama did not gain the presidency because of the internet, but it is questionable whether he could have defeated the crowded Democratic primary field without it. In this election, new technology proved itself on the biggest political stage, acting as a tool for communication, mobilisation and organisation.

In this chapter Jennifer Stromer-Galley examines the impact of the internet on the election campaign and, in particular, the new raft of interactive and multimedia technologies commonly referred to as 'web 2.0'. She charts how YouTube and viral video, social networking sites, text messaging, and microblogging sites such as Twitter all played their part in extending the various candidates' messages in new ways to new audiences.

This account holds three lessons for British progressives. First, centrally managed political spin is a far less effective weapon than it was a decade ago because the internet has democratised the range of news sources that people use. Second, we need to experiment with new technologies, and not expect to get it right first time. In the digital era, it is hard to predict exactly which niche site or social networking service will become 'the next big thing.' Instead, progressive groups must be present in a broad collection of online settings. Finally, online campaigning must not be viewed in isolation, but instead consciously linked to the offline world. This is what differentiated Obama's campaign from the innovative but flawed Dean campaign in 2004.

7. The web 2.0 election
Jennifer Stromer-Galley

On August 31st, 2006 Virginia Governor Mark Warner stepped foot into virtual reality, participating in an interview with a journalist via avatar in the virtual 'game' environment of Second Life. Warner, who entertained prospects of running in the Democratic presidential primaries, was exploring new ways of reaching possible voters.

This novel, early move in the 2008 presidential campaign season marked the start of many innovations with web 2.0 – the next generation of worldwide web applications that allows for greater user participation in generating content and in interaction with others than web 1.0. These innovations seem to have produced the kinds of effects that e-campaigners have been hoping for since 1996, when the first presidential campaign web sites were created.

Back then, I interviewed campaign staff who worked on the web sites of Republican presidential candidate Bob Dole and Democratic candidate Bill Clinton. In those interviews, it became clear that the worldwide web was viewed as *brochureware*. What they could not do was harness the internet's interactive capabilities, such as chat, message boards, or even e-mail. Campaign managers were deeply worried about the loss of control of the message that such increased interactivity with supporters and critics would entail, and they opted out of those capabilities.[1]

In 2008, we saw a markedly different landscape for presidential campaigns. web 2.0 was used to engage prospective voters through viral videos, social network sites, blogging and microblogging, and text messaging, and to let supporters engage in the campaigns by generating the content. In doing so, campaigns surrendered some of the control of their message they have historically held in a tight grip. The result for campaigns is a delicate balancing act between guiding the message and surrendering to the message constructed about them. When done effectively, it can lead to increased fundraising, name recognition and, most importantly, votes.

In this chapter a few of the innovations in web 2.0 technology are described, and the pros and cons for campaigns are considered.

YouTube and viral video

YouTube transformed the way campaigns think about video. No longer were they solely thinking about television advertising; now, they also had to think about videos for YouTube and for their own campaign web sites. Campaigns hired staff whose job was primarily to travel with the campaign shooting video of candid, behind-the-scenes footage of the candidate and staff, and to shoot videos of the supporters, their testimonies, and their excitement about the campaign. Yet, those videos generally were not what went 'viral', the hot new word of this presidential campaign. As a marketing term, 'viral' connotes an idea that is spread – often through word-of-mouth rather than mass-mediated campaigns – and that has some benefit for the company, product or person at the core of the idea. For presidential campaigns in 2008, one of the primary goals was to create or to be the beneficiary of viral marketing.

There were several noteworthy viral videos worth examining in some detail.

- In March of 2007, the first viral video of the primary campaign appeared on YouTube. The 'Vote Different' video was a parody of an ad aired in 1984 that introduced the Macintosh PC. The original ad – itself a parody of George Orwell's dark totalitarian tale *1984* – depicted featureless and same-dressed men marching and then sitting in militaristic rows as a man on a massive video monitor heralds the anniversary of the dawn of pure ideology. A short, blonde woman wearing bright orange running shorts dashes into the theatre and throws a sledgehammer at the screen, freeing the masses from their indoctrination. In the 2007 ad, the video monitor footage is replaced with a video of Hillary Clinton in which she invites her viewers to start a conversation with her. The same runner wears an Obama t-shirt over her orange running shorts and throws the sledgehammer at the monitor. Text appears on the screen proclaiming that the 2008 election won't be like *1984*, and to 'vote different'.

- Another viral video that rocketed quickly into the American public's consciousness was the 'Yes We Can' video created by the hip-hop group Black Eye Peas' lead singer will.i.am. He posted the four-and-a-half minute video on 2nd February 2008, featuring a star-studded cast singing along to Barack Obama's New Hampshire primary speech.

- And, who can forget Obama Girl? The video featured a sexy, buxom, long haired brunet, Amber Lee Ettinger, in a music video mooning over Obama in "I got a crush ... on Obama". The sexually provocative video received more than 12 million views on YouTube.

These viral videos can have positive effects for campaigns. Especially during the primary season, establishing name recognition is essential in raising money and gaining votes. Viral videos help promote such name recognition. They can also speak to particular demographics in ways that the candidates and campaigns themselves sometimes cannot. Although Obama was able to cross demographic barriers and speak to younger voters, many candidates find it a challenge to speak to young people. Viral videos can let young celebrities or wannabes speak to youth and raise a candidate's appeal in their eyes.

Such recognition and appeal also comes at a price. Viral videos are beyond the control of the campaign. Rarely are true viral videos generated from within. They're created by people with their own motives and messages, which may work at cross-purposes with the campaign. The ObamaGirl video contributed to the perception that Obama was a celebrity, on which he was attacked by his opponent John McCain in the general election.[2] The 'Vote Different' video caused controversy for the Obama campaign, posing a public relations challenge. In both instances they opted to provide little comment, which was the prudent approach to handling the videos while benefiting from their popularity and thereby contributing to Obama's growing fame.

Social networking sites

Another noteworthy innovation in the 2008 election was the widespread use of social networking sites, such as Facebook and MySpace, by campaigns and supporters. All of the major campaigns in the Democratic and Republican primaries created profiles of the candidates on these, and other, social networking sites.

Content on the social networking sites focused primarily on providing notes, similar to announcements, with updates about the campaign, links to videos and to photos, as well as brief biographical sketches, along with personal information such as birthdays, marital status, and favourite books and music.

One additional component of these social networking sites are the 'wall' or 'comment' feature wherein visitors to the profile leave a comment to the campaign or engage in a conversation with other visitors. This function is quite distinct from blog comments in that social networking site comments have no article or opinion to focus a conversation or comment. Instead, as Zube found, comments left on MySpace candidate profiles tended to be messages of support for the candidate, questions about how to further help the candidate, spam, or gratitude that the campaign 'friended' the visitor – allowing them to comment on the profile in the first place.[3]

Social networking profiles, on the face of it, do not seem to provide much benefit to campaigns, especially since they cannot mine information about visitors, as that information is owned by the social networking site, and interested people cannot become active on the profile by providing comments until a staff member or volunteer accepts their 'friend' request.

Yet, they did it. Why? Campaigns reported that they set up profiles because it provided another opportunity to connect with voters 'where they live.' Mike Soohoo, Deputy E-campaign Manager for the McCain team during the primary and general election, said in an interview that the primary objective of their social networking sites was to generate buzz, and to create the kind of viral media on the site, such as games that visitors could play, that would generate further traffic to the profile and subsequent support. These motives highlight the increased importance presidential campaigns placed on word-of-mouth testimony among friends to help generate interest in the campaign, in contrast with the more mass-mediated focused campaigns of past years.

Indeed, substantial buzz was generated about the candidates' social networking sites. Print and broadcast news stories featured the novel application of social networking in political campaigning. Such articles translated into free media for the campaign, in which enthusiastic supporters as well as the trendiness of the campaign were profiled. Along with viral marketing, these positive, free mass-mediated messages are a desirable secondary benefit for campaigns.

Not only did campaigns benefit from the free media, they also picked up new supporters – especially among young voters. Much noise was made about the role of the youth vote in the 2008 election, given that the candidates seemed to be communicating heavily where young people spend their mediated time. Obama, in particular, seemed to have mastered first, and most effectively, the online media environment. During the primaries and caucuses, 60 per cent of youth voters cast their vote for Obama, making youth voters an important part of his winning coalition.[4] Political elites are generally not aggressive in seeking the youth vote, primarily because they have little money and they are less likely to actually come to the polls on election day than older voters. Yet in the 2008 election, their presence was significant.

Other innovations

Two other innovations are worth mentioning, as they contributed to the overall technological landscape in the 2008 presidential campaign. The first was text messaging to cell phones. The second was microblogging.

SMS text messaging was used by campaigns for the first time in the 2008 election. Democratic primary candidate, and former vice presidential nominee, John

Edwards, used SMS to communicate with supporters. One of the difficulties with text messaging is acquiring phone numbers. During campaign rallies Edwards would hold up his cell phone and then ask his audience to do the same and then to text the campaign with the short code "HOPE". In this clever way, the campaign could collect telephone numbers.[5] Other campaigns soon followed the strategy.

The text messaging strategy that produced the most buzz, however, was Barack Obama's announcement that he would text message his vice presidential running mate pick. This produced heavy news coverage, and positive free media, as well as the desired cell phone numbers from interested followers of the Obama campaign.

The benefit of SMS is that recipients of texts are significantly more likely to open such messages and read them, especially as compared with email.[6] Thus, if campaigns really want supporters to pay attention to a message – a critical plea for money, a major campaign announcement – using SMS is a way to guarantee that the recipient will see it.

Microblogging is best known by the name of the company that created it, Twitter.com. Twitter allows users to send short 140 character messages into the ether for anyone who is 'following' them, called *tweets*. The campaign teams used Twitter throughout the race to make announcements about campaign events, locations of the candidate, and to provide URLs for giving contributions or reading articles or announcements. Of note, John Edwards, the first candidate to utilise Twitter, made policy positions and clarifications through it in dialogue with followers. Twitter was also popular with campaign staff who created personal Twitter accounts. Their use, however, at times bordered on the political, and with consequences. A McCain staffer used his personal Twitter account to send a message alerting followers to a video on

YouTube that edited footage from Reverend Wright's controversial sermons with speeches of Barack Obama's in an effort to publicise the video and attack the candidate. He was fired from the campaign for his message, as it violated the campaign's policy of banning attacks on Obama's former pastor.[7] Thus, even a relatively unknown and cutting edge technology was harnessed by campaigns in the 2008 election. This is remarkable given that blogging, for example, had been utilised as early as 1999 but campaigns did not adopt it until 2004, and then only after they saw the maverick candidate, Howard Dean, use it to great success.

Conclusion

What Americans saw in the 2008 presidential election was a remarkable amount of innovation and experimentation by presidential campaigns. Generally, they are prone to conservatism with new media, gingerly adapting to a new medium only after it has been proven effective. Of particular concern is the fear of losing control of the message.[8] On the other hand, experimentation that generates contributions and supporters is worth the risk. Campaigns in 2008 seemed to calculate the cost/benefit ratio differently, viewing that the loss of control was not as big of a concern as losing the opportunity to generate cash and votes.

Yet, having said that, none of the gadgets and tools matter if the enthusiasm and support generated online fails to translate into effective 'boots on the ground' political organizing, as the Howard Dean's 2004 primary campaign failure suggests. One example of this mobilisation is Students for Obama, which started as a Facebook group, and became a Political Action Committee, with all of the formal structures of a PAC, and over 60,000 members and chapters at 80 colleges.[9] These supporters not only used digital media to promote the candidate but also to organise. They used the technology to coordinate on-the-ground events, such as rallies, fundraisers, and get-out-the-vote efforts.[10] It is this move from online to offline, from candidate-centred message to citizen-supported campaigning, that makes new media an effective, integrated component of the campaign, and not simply a risky gimmick.

In this chapter, Faiz Shakir writes a short history of US political blogging and its role in the election. There are three lessons for progressive groups in the UK. First, blogging is more effective as a campaigning tool when it is used for 'rapid response research' – reacting quickly to statements, speeches and policies by conservatives, and publicising moments of hypocrisy, especially where the mainstream media reaction has been poor.

Second, bloggers can usefully exist outside the mainstream structures of a political party or campaign, giving them free license to go on the attack in a way that might diminish the reputation of politicians. This approach also gives the 'blogosphere' free reign to attack conservative positions by otherwise progressive politicians, as Obama himself found out in relation to intelligence surveillance legislation.

Finally, blogging provides a powerful communications tool through which politicians can connect with the public. The Speaker of the House of Representatives, Nancy Pelosi, provides a daily update of committee hearings, and congressional reports which would otherwise get lost by the media. Following the success of Barack Obama's social networking tool, my.barackobama.com, which connected supporters and became a source for local organisation, it is widely hoped he will be even more innovative in government. This could include providing bloggers with access to key personnel and information.

8. Blogging the election
Faiz Shakir

While a few weblogs began popping up at the turn of the 21st century, popularised blogging began as a political force in the 2004 election cycle. It was during the Bush vs. Kerry contest that bloggers first consistently created news that received widespread attention, began building large audiences, and – most importantly – started to organise and link to similarly-minded sites and stories.

Markos Moulitsas Zuniga, the founder of the Daily Kos, was an early blogging pioneer. He provided a voice of anti-war progressivism at a time when that perspective was rarely heard in the mainstream political debate. As a veteran, Moulitsas started his blog for, in his words, "personal therapy" to get his frustrations with the Bush administration off his chest.

The success of The Daily Kos is due to the site's unique, innovative model which empowered individuals to create their own diaries within the Daily Kos site. Cumulatively, these separate and independent bloggers formed a community around a common ideology and shared interests, and in turn, have generated a huge amount of traffic to the site. Visitors are drawn not only to the front page postings but also to 'recommended diarists' that are given mass approval by the site's community members. Other popular sites during this time were authored by journalists, such as Talking Points Memo by Joshua Micah Marshall and Andrew Sullivan's The Daily Dish.

During the 2004 election, I was involved in the Kerry campaign as a researcher at the Democratic National Committee. After Kerry lost, I was looking to build new skills and moved to the Center for American Progress, a think tank founded in 2003 by Bill Clinton's former chief of staff John Podesta. I joined the team which ran Think Progress, a start-up blog that was operating in its third month with approximately 200,000 visitors a month.

In contrast to the Daily Kos or Talking Points Memo model, we shied away from opinion pieces and established ourselves as the first 'rapid response research blog.' We saw an opportunity to use our think tank resources and research skills to carry out analysis in areas where the media was failing, publicising moments of hypocrisy and fact-checking misstatements by conservatives.

Over time, our traffic grew tremendously, receiving over six million visits in November 2008. With greater power came greater responsibility, and we began to enlarge the scope of our blogging activities. We evolved into a progressive news outlet. In addition to oppositional research, we began to inform a progressive audience about the stories they should care about on any given day. Among our many key issues from 2004 to 2008, we focused on Iraq, torture, corruption in Congress, and media failures.

The 2008 election

The 2008 election demonstrated the power that progressive bloggers have attained. By breaking stories of national prominence, bloggers began to drive the political narrative on a daily basis. Also, during this election cycle, traditional journalistic outlets began operating their own blogs, while prominent bloggers began doing original reporting. Innovators like Jed Lewinson, a former marketing executive at the leading internet media firm RealNetworks, utilised his skills to become particularly effective in demonstrating the utility of enhanced multimedia, slicing and dicing television footage to highlight contradictions or hypocrisy. The collective efforts of these bloggers provided new, interesting content that you could not find anywhere else.

The Huffington Post broke new ground by enlisting readers to become roving reporters. It is not yet clear whether this was an effective use of resources, but it did result in one of the most prominent stories of the campaign when a blogger recorded Barack Obama making a speech at a private fundraising event in San Francisco. Speaking about people from small towns in Pennsylvania and the Midwest, Obama said, "It's not surprising then they get bitter, they cling to guns or religion or antipathy to people who aren't like them or anti-immigrant sentiment or anti-trade sentiment as a way to explain their frustrations."[1] Indeed, nothing is private in the age of blogging. Hillary Clinton's campaign used the audio from this quote in political ads, helping propel her to victories in Pennsylvania and other predominantly white, blue-collar areas.

Because the pace of activity was so ferocious during the campaign, bloggers were better positioned than print journalists to be the first to report stories. The campaign teams were forced to read and react to blogs in order to stay in the loop and avoid missing all the key breaking stories that might cause them joy or pain.

Bloggers were able to drive a political debate when they joined together in linking to certain stories, quickly transforming them into common public knowledge. Network TV outlets would quote these blog posts, and campaigns were forced to respond directly to the postings. By the time the evening news aired each night, there were many more iterations of a story than in previous campaigns. TV shows like Countdown with Keith Olbermann on MSNBC or leading publications like Politico got many story ideas from the progressive blogosphere.

Consider the case of John McCain forgetting how many houses he owned. In previous campaigns, that would have been a one day print media story. But the blogosphere kept finding new angles to discuss the story, for instance, debating how many homes McCain really owned and why his wealth was an important policy story. Similarly, bloggers gleefully reminded readers of John McCain's candid admissions that US troops could be in Iraq for 100 years and the economy was not something he understood well. And bloggers propelled figures like McCain adviser Phil Gramm (who famously said the US was locked in a "mental recession") and phrases like "terrorist fist jab" (a comment by Fox News anchor ED Hill) to national prominence.

There is, however, an occasional downside to the blogosphere's role in amplifying certain news stories – namely, when they turn out to be untrue. One of the most prominent examples came after the election when Fox News reporter Carl Cameron reported that Sarah Palin was not aware that Africa was a continent. This story turned out to be a hoax, but the blogosphere had already clipped the video and disseminated it widely. Once the genie was out of the bottle, it was hard to correct readers' incorrect impressions.

But the blogosphere necessarily has lower standards of sourcing than traditional media outlets. Blogging is the art form of raw emotion, first reaction, and gut instinct. Using a literary metaphor, it is a rough draft, not the final hard cover copy. And the blogosphere is a true free market of information; it is up to individual bloggers to decide whether they give a particular story any credibility. Readers will reward sites that are reliable and consistent.

The relationship between the blogosphere and the Obama campaign was not as strong as people perceived from the outside. The common perception seems to be that the Obama campaign was aggressively enlisting bloggers to promote its cause. In reality, much of the progressive blogosphere registered its early support of the John Edwards campaign. Meanwhile, the Obama campaign focused its efforts on building its own progressive infrastructure through my.barackobama.com and did not prioritise blogger outreach. Perhaps the campaign realised that these bloggers would provide a helpful function regardless.

Nonetheless, the blogosphere creatively used MyBO.com for its own purposes. Mike Stark, an eclectic figure who had made his name in the blogosphere by phoning right-wing radio shows and challenging them with liberal views, was the architect of one of the most famous grassroots actions of the campaign. He opposed Obama's position of providing legal immunity for telecom companies that had participated in Bush's warrantless surveillance program. He set up a MyBO.com profile and enlisted over 23,000 other members in an appeal for Obama to "get FISA [Foreign Intelligence Surveillance Act] right."[1] Although Obama did not change his position in response to the protest, he was ultimately compelled to engage in the debate by sending a message to the petitioners outlining why he had made his choice.

A final example of the blogosphere's power was its ability to spawn new political pundits. Nathaniel 'Nate' Silver, the founder of polling analysis site FiveThiryEight.com, was unknown before the election. He rose to prominence by blogging his criticisms of mainstream polling organisations, critiquing their methods, and providing alternative polling analyses. He was proven to be more accurate than these organisations and predicted, for example, that Obama would win a landslide victory over Hillary Clinton in the North Carolina primary. Silver's final forecast accurately predicted the winner of 49 of the 50 states (Indiana being the exception). His forecast of a 6.1 percentage point margin for Obama in the combined national popular vote was just 0.9 away from the actual winning margin of 7.0 points.[2]

Similarly, Rachel Maddow, who calls herself a "blogger on TV," emerged as a leading MSNBC political commentator and later the anchor of her own show based in part on her popularity in the progressive blogosphere. Throughout the 2008 campaign, bloggers on both the left (like Ezra Klein) and right (like Michelle Malkin) appeared as frequent TV analysts. As the popular journalist-blogger Ben Smith has noted, the once substantial barriers between the "MSM" (mainstream media) and the blogosphere have become quite porous as a result of the latest presidential cycle.[3]

Some lesser-known rising stars of the progressive blogosphere – like anti-coal blogger Kevin Grandia, and Iraq and Afghanistan war veteran Brandon Friedman – also gained a foothold in 2008 by covering niche issues.[4] In doing so, they have established themselves as leading issue advocates.

Going forward

With a popular, progressive, and pragmatic president in the White House, there are two potentially complementary pathways for the blogosphere to proceed. First, they may embrace the role of holding President Obama's feet to the fire on key issues. The progressive blogosphere cares deeply about issues such as ending the war in Iraq, ending torture, addressing climate change, enacting universal healthcare, and closing Guantanamo Bay. The blogosphere will undoubtedly hold Obama to his campaign promises on these and other issues.

If a professional conservative blogosphere emerges, it may also play an important role in holding Obama to account. That said, the conservative blogosphere to date has been largely ineffective in driving political stories and has instead been marked by opinion-based ranting. With the exception of the National Review and Malkin's Hot Air, there are few in the conservative realm undertaking intensive reporting, research, or fact checking. Thus, in this new progressive era, there is an opportunity for conservative blogs to emerge as leading voices for the opposition.

The other possibility is for the Obama administration to work more closely with the progressive blogosphere than it did during the campaign, and make it an integral part of its communications strategy. Speaker Nancy Pelosi already operates a valuable blog which is used to publish video and provide citizens with information about Congress's activities. It is hoped that Barack Obama will do something similar for the Executive Branch. By giving bloggers access to key personnel and information, Obama could use the internet as a powerful tool to drive his agenda and engage in conversations with large audiences on a daily basis. Nevertheless, there are many within Congress and Obama's team who remain sceptical about working with the blogosphere out of fear of what this unregulated and ungoverned space might produce. Although the blogosphere's role as an important electioneering tool is now secured, it remains to be seen whether 2008 will truly mark a watershed moment in its relationship with the levers of power.

In this chapter, Matthew McGregor outlines how campaign finance in the 2008 election became a democratising rather than a corrupting force. The sheer number of people who donated, and the relatively small amounts that they gave, were critical to Obama's success in building a multi-million member movement.

Obama's campaign saw fundraising as an integral part of its outreach to supporters rather than a separate element of the campaign. For example, requests for donations were interlinked with information about rallies or canvassing events.

Despite the differences between British and American political culture and the campaign finance environment, there are lessons for those who wish to emulate Obama's success. First, form a personal relationship with your supporters, tailoring emails to their specific needs and interests. Second, do not treat your supporters like a cash register and make sure to involve them in activities at the same time as asking for money. Finally, adapt and innovate by, for example, testing different techniques and designs on your web site to see what works best.

9. The democratising force of fundraising
Matthew McGregor

The 2008 election was remarkable in many ways, but one aspect of the contest that will continue to reverberate is the success achieved by presidential candidates as political fundraisers. In total, the candidates raised more than $1.7 billion during the cycle.[1] This staggering figure was driven partly by the money-focused US political system. But it was also based on extremely skilful campaigning, which persuaded millions of Americans to part with their hard-earned cash to support the candidates in whom they believed.

The Obama campaign proved to be especially adept at this aspect of electoral politics, raising more than $657 million.[2] This was nearly double the amount raised by John McCain, and allowed Obama to become the first ever candidate to refuse public funding for the general election campaign.

Obama's fundraising broke new ground in two key ways. First, he was able to recruit a huge army of donors who tended to give small amounts of money repeatedly throughout the campaign. In total, of the 6.5 million donations made, more than 90 per cent were less than $100. Secondly, he was able to tap into the fundraising potential of the internet. He was not the first candidate to do this – McCain in 2000 and Dean in 2004 both had good online fundraising, with Dean raising a then-record of $27 million online – but the sheer volume raised by Obama was on an unprecedented scale, totalling more than $500 million.[3]

How was this achieved? In order to understand why Obama was so successful with small donors and online fundraising, and what lessons these hold for British politics, a good starting point is to examine one specific event – a moment in time where the course of the election hung in the balance and fundraising was to play a hugely important role.

The September 2007 funding deadline

In September 2007, the Illinois Senator's campaign was facing a make-or-break moment. Hillary Clinton was almost 20 points ahead in the national polls, and Obama was lagging behind in the critical state of Iowa. What is more, the quarterly filing deadline, when candidates had to report their latest fundraising figures to the Federal Election Commission, was approaching. Having good numbers would prove that a candidate was a real contender, while underperformance could mortally wound a campaign's hopes. A few days before the filing deadline, Michelle Obama forwarded an email from her husband to the million or so supporters then on the campaign email list, asking them to donate. Michelle Obama's email wasn't a desperate plea for money, though. It was a short, personal message focused on mobilising the grassroots to change politics and America. In it, she wrote:

> "When Barack and I discussed this campaign and what it would mean for our family, we agreed it would only be worth doing if we left the political process better off than how we found it – not for just our family, but for the country and for folks around the world."

This was genuinely people-powered fundraising, an idea that was reflected in the goal that the Obama team set themselves. Instead of aiming for a specific amount – say

$1 million in a day – they wanted 250,000 individual donors to give before the deadline. It was about the number of people joining in, and not about the amount that they gave. The Obama campaign prioritised the movement over the money, but worked in the knowledge that if a successful movement was built, the money would surely follow.

The campaign did not rely wholly on the internet in the run up to the deadline. The message from Michelle Obama was part of a broader series of campaign events, built around a rally in Washington Square Park in Manhattan at the end of the month. This was the result of several weeks of planning, and allowed supporters to get involved in a number of ways. Those resident in New York were asked to invite friends and colleagues to attend, or to organise transport or accommodation for those visiting for the rally. In parallel, supporters around the country were encouraged to hold their own events, linked to the main activity. All this was covered extensively on the campaign blog, the Obama YouTube channel, and through a constant stream of emails. On the night itself, the rally was streamed live using a portable aircard connection on a staffer laptop. In this one rally, supporters could engage with the campaign in a range of different ways.

The end result of these efforts turned out to be remarkable. Obama raised $19 million in the third quarter of 2007 and recruited 140,000 completely new donors who had never given to his campaign before. While this was less than Hillary Clinton's $22 million for that quarter, it showed the Illinois Senator was a serious contender, with a genuine chance of winning the nomination.[4]

The Obama fundraising model

Understanding why supporters responded so strongly in September 2007 is the key to understanding how Obama for America raised $657 million, and how it propelled

Obama to the White House. This success had a number of aspects.

First, campaign finance-related issues were integral to the overall relationship between the campaign and supporters. They were not seen as a standalone task to be carried out in isolation from the rest of the effort. This was reflected in the structure of the campaign – there cannot be one silo for canvass teams, another for media work, and yet another for raising donations. Such an approach would create the danger that the various aims of a campaign compete with rather than complement each other. Instead, an integrated method also meant that every aspect of an individual supporter's commitment to the campaign, financial or otherwise, was seen as important and is joined into a wider strategy.

Second, the campaign worked hard to construct a genuine relationship with each of its supporters. The seeds of this relationship could be the tiniest piece of information, maybe an email address or a mobile phone number. In order to get these details, the campaign had to offer something in return. Sometimes this was exclusive information, which the campaign gave to supporters before anyone else. Most famously, this happened in the case of the vice presidential nomination announcement, where citizens could sign up to be the first to know the name of the running mate. By attempting to bypass the media and demonstrating the centrality of supporters, this idea fitted in well with the campaign's overall approach. Additionally though, the campaign was able to secure the email or mobile details of more than a million people keen to be the first to hear the news – people not previously in the campaign's orbit.

Once a citizen has been contacted, they have become part of the movement, and therefore it becomes critical for the campaign to engage them as much as possible. Technology was central to this process. The Obama campaign had a strong foundation here – online tools that are easily adapted as circumstances change, and which didn't collapse, even when millions of people were trying to access them. However, it would be easy to misunderstand this, and take an overly techno-centric view of Obama's success. There was no 'build it and they will come' mentality – but a genuine and authentic desire to place in supporters' hands the tools to make Barack Obama president – and one of those tools was the ability to donate, and donate often.

Various techniques were employed to construct the relationships within the movement. The simplest of these was email. The Obama campaign used its list to reach out to people personally, and ask things of them that were focused on the moment – on that week or month in the campaign. The email list itself contained over 13.5 million addresses, but they were heavily segmented to allow the campaign to hone the message to different groups of people, depending on their location, their level of activism, the amount they had donated, and dozens of other criteria. As a result of this, over two years, the campaign sent more than 7000 unique emails.

The content of the emails was also important. As with the communications sent before the New York rally, requests for donations were always interlinked with other important activities – whether that was attending an event, working at a local campaign office, putting up a young field organiser living away from home, making phone calls through the campaign's online phone bank, forwarding a video or joining a door knocking session. All of these activities, without distinction, were investments in the outcome of the campaign.

In addition to email, the campaign developed and honed a series of facilities that encouraged supporters to give. One such tool was a 'match donations' feature. Supporters, especially those who had not yet made their first donation, were paired with another supporter who had agreed to match their sum. To make it more personal, the two donors were able to exchange notes on why they were donating and supporting the Obama campaign.

Since supporters in their local communities were the campaign's best advocates, they were given the tools to reach out to their close friends and family, and organise their own fundraising drives. One of the tools on my.barackobama.com ('MyBO') allowed supporters to raise money directly from their friends and family, and to show how much they had individually brought in to the campaign. Through their own profile page, supporters could send emails to their contacts asking for donations, and people giving in response to these messages had their donations tagged, so they would appear on the profile page of the supporter who made the ask.

Another of the MyBO tools allowed supporters to create their own local events easily, whether they were debate parties, bake sales, or a pre-convention celebration. This also allowed activists to associate a donation request or entry fee with the event, streamlining the traditional local fundraising initiatives and lowering the bar to organising these events by reducing the work needed.

Putting tools in the hands of supporters so that they can use their own personal relationships to help the campaign, and get the credit for their work highlights the underlying principles of the campaign very clearly: we provide the tools, you provide the network, everyone wins.

Conclusion

Quoting Martin Luther King during the inaugural celebrations, Obama said "change does not roll in on the wheels of inevitability." The same could be said of his campaign. It would be all too easy to think that Obama's fundraising success occurred as if by magic. But such an assumption would be false. It was in fact the product of a long and careful process to think of the best ways to empower supporters and construct a relationship with them.

Furthermore, this process was ongoing. The design of the tools on the Obama campaign web site was continuously evolving, modifying every conceivable variable, including the language used on the page, the use of other media, such as video, and even the colour and position of the donate button. Experimentation was not feared, and the immediacy of online communications and donations gave the campaign the opportunity to measure and optimise every variable.

The dividends of this approach were huge, and were certainly much greater than the sheer quantity of money raised (vital though that was). Donations to political parties and candidates are often associated in the public imagination with corruption, or the powerful and wealthy trying to buy influence. Yet this was different. Every giver to Obama became an integral member in his campaign team. Giving in this way was not the opposite of traditional activism, but a hugely important part of it. When people gave money, they were forging a relationship with a movement which led them to do more, not less. That is genuine people-powered politics.

*Yair Ghitza and Todd Rogers explain how the statistical tech-
niques of microtargeting and randomised controlled experiments have improved the effectiveness of campaigns. As a
result of recent innovations, two tasks that are as old as democracy itself – predicting each citizen's political preferences, and
determining how best to influence them – have become more
accurate and cheaper to do.*

*Improved and consolidated databases, better political infor-
mation, more experienced practitioners, and wider use of experimentation all improved progressives' ability in 2008 to target
and communicate with voters. For example, experiments have
shown that door-to-door contact is more effective at increasing
turnout than telephone canvassing or mail shots. Experiments
have also found that text messaging is especially effective for
increasing yturnout, which was an innovation widely used by
the Obama campaign.*

*Although legal restrictions in the UK appear to limit the
utility of these techniques, much can be replicated using
existing sources such as granular census data and information gained from canvassing operations. Ultimately, Ghitza
and Rogers argue, these techniques improve both candidates'
relationships with voters and their likelihood of victory.*

10. Data-driven politics
Yair Ghitza and Todd Rogers

Anyone who has ever been part of a political campaign knows that which voters get targeted depends on two simple questions. What are each citizen's political preferences? And what will change them? These preferences refer to an individual's beliefs about a candidate or issue, and ultimately who they will support in an election. They can also refer to actions like donating money, volunteering, turning out to cast a vote, or attending a rally.

Traditionally, these questions have been answered with polling, educated guesswork, and on-the-doorstep experience. While each of these has a place in politics, they are incomplete. Polling provides excellent snapshots of the beliefs and preferences of the electorate as a whole, or even, to some extent, subgroups of the electorate. It cannot, however, tell us about the beliefs and preferences of each specific individual, and it is imprecise in telling us how best to change those beliefs and preferences. Educated guesswork and experience can help us avoid many mistakes, but they cannot provide unambiguous guidance.

Recent advances in data-driven politics offer dramatic improvements in our ability to answer these questions. Two specific innovations enable much greater efficiency and precision in contacting voters by combining information about individuals' preferences and their likelihoods of changing their minds with national political strategies. The first innovation is microtargeting; the second is the use of randomised control experiments to determine which type of contact and wording will most cost-effectively change a voter's beliefs and actions. We look at each in turn.

Microtargeting

Microtargeting is the statistical analysis of large-scale databases to help campaigns and organisations determine the beliefs and expected actions of individuals. This involves the analysis of publicly available data such as voter registration, demographic and census information, party registration, whether they voted in previous elections, and information collected directly from an individual, for example, from canvassing. These databases are combined with survey data to create statistical models which predict each citizen's political beliefs and the likelihood of their taking specific actions. Although all predictions are constrained by the limits of statistical inference, these techniques significantly increase an analysts' ability to predict a citizen's political preferences.

While microtargeting was used by some progressive organisations prior to 2004, major advances in sophistication and in its adoption were made in the 2006 midterm elections and in the 2008 presidential election. The improvements can be traced to three changes. First, the data infrastructure has been improved and consolidated. Today, there are two main voter file databases in progressive politics – one at the Democratic National Committee, and one at Catalist, a private vendor. In contrast to earlier years when voter file collection was handled on a campaign-by-campaign basis, and required significant and repeated start up costs, this centralised infrastructure allows campaigns to develop microtargeting models using data of better quality and broader scope than in the past with much less difficulty.

Second, developing a centralised data infrastructure has allowed organisations to collect and track meaningful political information about voters. This includes the preferences, beliefs, and actions of individuals as collected over the phone, at voters' doors, and however else possible. Since microtargeting models can only incorporate the data that is available, early microtargeting relied heavily on information like voter history and demographic information provided by commercial vendors and the US Census. By accumulating and centralising useful political information, more recent microtargeting models have had even greater predictive power. Importantly, the collection of political information builds on campaigns' natural strengths, especially those with strong grassroots organizing capabilities. In the past, campaigns could learn about individual voters and use the information accordingly, but after the election they would often lose track of the data. Today, all of this information is saved for the use of future progressive campaigns.

Third, increased experience with the analysis of large datasets by members of the progressive community has improved the quality and adoption of microtargeting. The statistical procedures used in microtargeting have long been used in academia, business, and other realms. But translating these tools to the new domain of politics took time because of three problems: using polls and voter files together is complex because bias exists in both data sources; the steady accumulation of talented data analysts took time; and there was a need to communicate to end-users how to effectively use microtargeting to achieve their goals.

In the 2008 election there was an explosion in the use of microtargeting to more efficiently contact voters. For example, people who were predicted to be highly likely

Kerry and allies

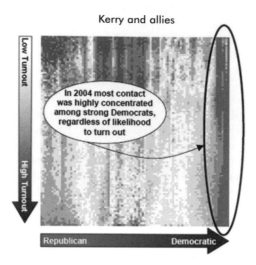

Obama and allies

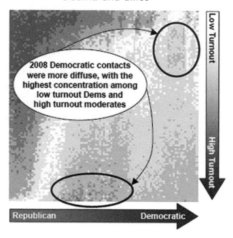

Figure 4: Ohio Contacts – 2004 vs. 2008. *This figure shows how Kerry only targeted Democrats, while Obama targeted both low turnout Democrats and high turnout independents.*[4]

to vote but only moderately likely to support the Democrats ('high-turnout, swing voters') were contacted for purposes of persuasion. And citizens who were only moderately likely to vote but highly likely to support Democrats ('moderate turnout, Dem voters') were targeted to ensure that they actually voted. Figure 4 illustrates that these two groups were much more precisely targeted by Obama and allies than by Kerry and allies in 2004. This data is based on Catalist's recorded voter contacts in Ohio during these two elections. While contact by the Kerry campaign was intense among high-turnout Democrats – who are probably good targets for activism, volunteer-recruitment and fundraising purposes – Obama's campaign focused considerably more on the two groups described above.

In addition to the top-level targeting displayed in Figure 4, microtargeting helps campaigns identify the specific issues which individuals care about. For example, an environmental or pro-choice group can use microtargeting to help identify voters favourable to their issues.

Randomised control experiments

While microtargeting helps determine current political preferences, randomised control experiments (RCE) provide guidance on how best to change voter's minds. RCEs are widely used by pharmaceutical companies to evaluate the true causal impact of new drugs and increasingly by businesses to determine what maximises profit and what does not. Recent business press books like Competing on Analytics and Supercrunchers have discussed how companies like Amazon.com and Capital One have built RCEs into their core business models. Capital One, for example, conducted more than 25,000 RCEs in 2005 alone.

To make an RCE work, each individual must be randomly assigned to either a treatment group or a control group. Because each individual has an equal probability of being assigned to any one group, the population of people assigned to each of the conditions can be assumed to be identical in all ways measurable (such as age or gender, for example) and all ways that are not so easily measured (maybe their favourite news source, or the number of hours spent on the internet). At this point, one can expose each group to a different treatment (or none at all for the control group). One then collects whatever measurement one is interested in from the individuals within each group. Any difference in this measure can be attributed to the treatment, since that was the only aspect that differed between conditions.

RCEs were first used in politics to understand the causal impact of different modes of voter contact a decade ago by two professors at Yale University, Alan Gerber and Don Green.[1] They were interested in what type of get-out-the-vote contact generated the greatest increase in turnout. Subsequent research has confirmed their initial finding that face-to-face contact has a greater impact on turnout than either phone calls or mail. Since that initial research, new studies have been conducted by academics and practitioners alike. One recent experiment found that get-out-the-vote messages sent via text message can be surprisingly powerful in increasing turnout, while emails have essentially no impact.[2]

In light of this research, it was not surprising that the Obama campaign focused so intensively throughout their campaign on collecting cell phone numbers and using them to communicate with their supporters. For example, in the lead-up to the announcement of their pick for vice president, the Obama campaign let its supporters know that the announcement would be made over text message. They used the opportunity to collect the cell phone numbers of supporters, and subsequently integrated text messaging as a valuable part of their get-out-the-vote plan. Understanding why text messages work but emails, for example, do not is not well understood. In the meantime, the practical implications are clear – and the Obama campaign seemed to act on them.

Once an organisation has chosen a mode of contact, it is still left to determine what to say and to whom. RCEs are a powerful tool for identifying which specific messages can change political preferences. The most widely discussed example was conducted by the AFL-CIO, a large labour union. They were interested in which mail shot would have the greatest impact in reducing support for McCain among their members. They developed three different pieces of literature and sent each one to a randomly selected group of 20,000 members in Ohio. Another randomly selected group of 20,000 Ohio members received no mail (the control group). The AFL-CIO then conducted a survey of the political preferences of the members in all four conditions. Figure 5 shows that

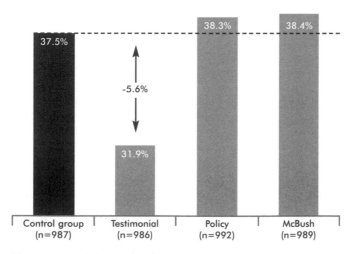

Figure 5: AFL-CIO Membership Mail Test in March 2008 (Percentage of each group intending to vote for McCain)[5]

two of the three pieces of mail had no meaningful impact on vote choice relative to the control group. At the same time, the third leaflet (the 'testimonial' piece) showed a statistically significant and meaningful decrease in McCain support. This was surprising given that all three designs were developed using the best information and methods available at the time. The AFL-CIO was then able to mail the testimonial piece to the rest of its Ohio universe knowing that it worked, and was potent.

As well as being effective stand alone tools, microtargeting and RCEs can also be used effectively together. For example, a recent 'meta-analysis' of more than a dozen get-out-the-vote RCEs conducted by Professors David Nickerson (Notre Dame University) and Kevin Arceneaux (Temple University) found that individuals, whom microtargeting models suggest have a moderate to low likelihood of voting in a given election, show the greatest boost in turnout as a result of face-to-face contact.[3] This finding was used to inform the get-out-the-vote targeting of many data-driven progressive organisations in this election cycle.

Microtargeting and RCEs for the Labour Party?

In applying these lessons to the UK, the most striking difference is the greater level of legal restriction on the use of personal data in the UK. In the US, much more individual-level information is available either freely or for purchase, including party registration and in which specific elections each citizen voted. But despite these limitations there are two other types of data that can still be of substantial value. First, granular census data at the local-level has been a potent (though imperfect) input for predicting individual-level demographic attributes in the US, and would probably have similar value in the UK. Second, as the Labour Party is already doing, individual political information such as candidate and issue preferences can be collected directly through grassroots activity, and is therefore ripe for microtargeting and RCEs.

On top of the legal hurdles, there are obvious ethical considerations about the collection and maintenance of such a large-scale database of personal information. The danger of improper use, both intentional and unintentional, is real. In the progressive community in the US, we are especially attuned to these concerns, and safeguarding against any type of violation has been a top priority. These safeguards, of course, should also be a top priority for any system built in the UK.

In the end, data-driven politics improves a campaign's ability to communicate effectively by anticipating and addressing what voters care about. Far from depersonalising politics, data-driven campaigning can actually improve a campaign's relationship with voters by helping them speak directly to the preferences and concerns of each individual citizen. If a campaign has a compelling vision and set of values, a long-term investment in data infrastructure can enable more efficient communication between a campaign and the electorate, and ultimately help win elections.

*While most of the public were focused on the presidential con-
test, the Democrats also did well in both the House of
Representatives and the Senate. Building on successes in the
2006 midterm elections, they won a number of districts and
states that had been Republican strongholds. One such success
was Glenn Nye's victory in Virginia's 2nd Congressional
District. In this chapter Representative Nye, with Robert Gerber,
offers a deeply personal account of his campaign for Congress.*

*These insights are important because a congressional dis-
trict is the environment that most closely resembles a British
parliamentary seat, much more so than the electoral college
system used in the race for the White House. Of course there
are differences. For example, the Nye campaign raised $1.2
million, largely to fund television advertising. But what is
most striking is that the bread and butter of constituency campaigning in both Britain and America remains shoe leather politics, knocking on doors and talking to voters.*

*As his chapter reveals, one of the great successes of the Nye
campaign was integrating this traditional form of politics with
more modern techniques. Email, for example, was used to create a network of highly active supporters and to rapidly rebut
false accusations made by his opponent. At the local level, new
communication technology need not be alienating to activists
or used at the expense of older forms of campaigning. Instead,
it can and must complement what already happens.*

11. Campaigning for Congress
Rep. Glenn Nye with Robert Gerber

In late 2007, I was one of many foreign development professionals working in Iraq. One day I found myself crouched in a bunker with some soldiers as the alarms for incoming mortars rang out through the dusty Baghdad air. As we waited for the 'all clear' to sound, the soldiers shared their concerns about what their families faced at home – the struggle to make ends meet, and partisan bickering in Washington that gave little hope for real solutions. I was struck by the fact that the soldiers worried more about America than they did about their physical safety in Iraq.

Service has always been a major part of my life. As a student, I used my vacations to help my physician father on medical missions overseas. After college, I passed the US State Department's Foreign Service exam and was stationed as a diplomat in the Balkans and Singapore. After the bunker discussion, I began to think about embarking on a new kind of public service.

Having returned home to Norfolk, Virginia for Christmas 2007, I began to explore what many advised was a crazy idea: running for the US House of Representatives. As a political novice with no name recognition and no money, it was not clear whether I had any chance of winning my home district. In every contest from 1998 to 2004, 98 per cent of incumbents in the House of Representatives won their election.[1] But although I was not known to be particularly political or partisan, I hoped that my ideas about bringing change to Washington would resonate with voters.

Virginia's 2nd Congressional District consists of three landmasses separated by water, and connected by bridges, covering the area commonly known as 'Hampton Roads'. The population of 640,000 includes the cities of Virginia Beach, Norfolk, and Hampton, and stretches from the Chesapeake Bay to the border of North Carolina. (The Jamestown settlement, the oldest in today's United States, is just a few miles north of the 2nd District.) Aside from a vast peninsula that forms Virginia's remote and rural Eastern Shore, the area is primarily urban and suburban, with the kind of sprawl to which Americans are accustomed. VA-2 is the East Coast home of the US Navy, hosting shipyards, nuclear-powered carriers, and the Oceana Naval Air Station – where the Navy until recently flew the F-14 Tomcats seen in the movie 'Top Gun.' Over 50 per cent of the 2nd District's residents have served in the US military. The district's population is diverse, with 20 per cent African-American population, and features opulent waterfront homes as well as pawn shops and trailer parks. Virginia Beach is also a vacation destination, with vast beaches, boardwalks, and fresh seafood.

After consulting some professional consultants on the viability of running for Congress, I set up an exploratory committee and began to raise money, one call at a time. The central task of any challenger in US politics is raising cash and building a fundraising base. Congressional races normally cost over $1 million. The money allows a candidate to hire a small team (in my case five full timers) and run TV advertisements. Given the size of the district, it becomes impossible to meet every resident. TV ads are the primary method of connecting with voters and establishing 'name ID'. Advertisements cost over $10,000 per week in a media market such as Norfolk's. The EMILY principal applies to campaigns in America – Early Money is Like Yeast. The early money is hard to raise, but the more you raise, the more people take you seriously and donate. Quarterly fundraising reports are public information so there is also a public relations aspect to the challenge. Ultimately, the majority of any candidate's time is set aside for fundraising calls – first to friends, then to individuals with a history of supporting like-minded candidates.

Late in 2007, my campaign commissioned a poll to help paint a picture of the issues that mattered most to local voters. The results showed that my professional record as an independent problem-solver, who had served in Iraq and understood foreign and defence policy, would resonate. Polling also showed that the incumbent, Republican Representative Thelma Drake, was vulnerable.

After declaring my candidacy in January 2008, my first task was to win the Democratic Party's nomination. I became a full-time candidate for Congress, and spent the next 10 months working 12 hour days, seven days per week. In the first few months of the campaign, I established some momentum by raising $200,000. By June, the filing deadline for potential candidates, no other Democrat had joined the race so the nomination was mine. At this stage I recruited a media consultant, a finance director to lead the fundraising drive, and my personal staff.

Part of the difficulty in beating incumbents is name recognition. In March, polls showed that Thelma Drake was known by 90 per cent of the district's residents while just 10 per cent knew my name. We didn't run TV ads until the fall, so name recognition was earned early on by grassroots outreach and positive press stories (known as 'earned media').

I knew I could take no voters for granted, so I pursued a geographically and demographically diverse outreach strategy. I was invited to speak at civic leagues, neighbourhood association picnics, veterans' association halls, and churches. I ate hot peppers at the Ethiopian-American New Year's Celebration in September and visited the local gun club (I prefer the 9mm Beretta). Meeting voters is easily the best part of the campaign and everyone I met had advice: "You need to put up more yard signs" or "You need to come to my school and speak." At big events, such as the local harbour festival, my loyal volunteers handed out flyers while I shook hands. The flyers featured key details from my biography and my campaign narrative. I emphasised my record of service in hotspots like Iraq and Afghanistan and my unyielding belief that bi-partisan solutions are the only way to solve problems in Washington. The campaign's strategy for success relied on 'staying on message', which meant incorporating these themes into debates, TV ads, and speeches.

During the course of the campaign, my opponent launched two unsubstantiated and inaccurate personal attacks against me, which attempted to portray me as untrustworthy. This required some rapid work to highlight the lies and reassure voters. My campaign web site had allowed supporters to sign up to an email service detailing campaign events and messages. My brother – who also served in Iraq as a civilian aid worker – sent out a message to recipients dismissing the allegations and outlining that it was another example of the same old divisive Washington politics that I sought to end. We also used that message to ask whether supporters would, "help us stand up against our opponent's empty attacks by donating \$25, \$50, \$100 or \$250 today". The appeal worked.

By contrast to Drake's adverts, mine focused on my biography, and the only criticism of my opponent focused on her voting record which included opposition to a crucial Act which supported education benefits for our district's servicemen and women. Through a combination of media coverage, voter outreach, and TV ads, my name recognition climbed steadily. By July, the local newspaper was calling our race "one of the region's most competitive".[2]

A third round of polling showed the race tightening. At this point I began to receive the endorsement of many leading Democrats in Virginia including Mark Warner who was running in the US Senate race. Meanwhile, Senator Obama's campaign was moving at full speed to register new voters and set up a grass-roots network. Virginia was a battleground state for Obama – which he went onto win – and so he made three visits to the district during the final month of the campaign. I was invited to speak before the presidential candidate at his rallies on these occasions. It was a complete thrill to address a cheering crowd of 20,000 who so clearly wanted to hear a message of change.

To win the district, I needed to win over independent voters and some Republicans. I have always been politically moderate and have no time for partisan bickering. I favour low taxes, support for small business, and a strong defence capability. My experience in Iraq and Afghanistan also helped convince military voters and folks who were concerned about the challenges America faces in an uncertain world. I also think my message of bipartisan solutions contrasted with the partisanship most voters saw in Washington. Meanwhile, Thelma Drake's association with President Bush – she was in the top 10 per cent of conservative representatives – came to haunt her as the nationwide financial and housing crises escalated.[3]

The election for the House of Representatives was third on the ballot, below the presidential election between Obama and McCain, and the Senatorial race between two former Governors, the Democrat Mark Warner and the Republican Jim Gilmore. But I simply could not take for granted that an Obama voter or a Warner voter would automatically vote for me, and so we organised our own field operation. This involved asking volunteers to host 'house parties' where I would discuss issues with a group of 20-30 undecided voters (occasionally while enjoying some home-cooked treats). We used these occasions to recruit new volunteers and collect donations as well. The second aspect of field operations was voter contact in key 'swing' precincts via phone, mail, and door-to-door canvassing every weekend during the final month. My campaign staff assembled a team of volunteers to execute the voter contact operation.

Modern campaigning tools had a more modest impact for my local campaign than for the presidential election but we still had to ensure that we were up to date. Supporters could donate online and databases owned by the state-wide Democratic Party were used to identify potential supporters using sophisticated logarithms. Nonetheless, in local politics you cannot beat the old techniques of TV, radio, and direct voter contact to build support.

Once the race had tightened considerably, the national party recorded and ran TV ads supporting me. Campaign finance rules, however, prevented my team from knowing the content of the ads before they aired. The Democratic National Committee's expenditures in the 2nd District for me exceeded $500,000. In addition, we had raised (and spent) over $1.2 million by election day. Thelma Drake had raised just over $2 million.[4]

The local press began following the race in earnest during the final two months of the campaign. I held a series of press conferences to highlight key issues, including energy costs or the urgency of veterans care issues. During this period I met with the editorial boards of the two local newspapers. The *Virginian-Pilot* gave me an unequivocal endorsement.[5]

In the end, I won by 12,000 votes – 53 per cent to 47 per cent. I am honoured by the responsibility that the people of the 2nd District have placed in me. The experience of defeating an incumbent and bringing a new style of politics to the area was immensely rewarding. But the real work has only just begun.

12. Conclusion
Nick Anstead and Will Straw

What does the Labour Party believe its role should be in the 21st century? Is it satisfied that a political party can be merely a means to electoral victory and therefore to subsequent achievements such as the foundation of the NHS or the creation of the minimum wage? Or should it aim to be more than that?

For progressives, successful political parties must be both a means *and* an end, playing a critical role in creating a vibrant space for civic participation and deliberation. This is a fundamental part of the constitutional left's definition of the good society, because apathy and disengagement are the enemy of progress and the nursemaids of reaction – the antithesis of what we seek to achieve. We believe that the Labour Party must, once again, become the spiritual home of the broad left and all those committed to a progressive – rather than a conservative – future.

As the authors in this book demonstrate, Barack Obama's victory suggests that increased participation and a situation where citizens feel that politics matters and take an active part in fighting for what they believe is compatible with, and increasingly important to, modern politics. Many facets of the Obama campaign are, of course, uniquely American, and made possible by the political culture and institutions in the United States. It is very unlikely that British parties, especially Labour twelve years into government, will be able to replicate the scale or intensity of enthusiasm that Obama generated (itself partly a product of eight years of reactionary, unilateral government).

But the American election does hold vital lessons that political parties must learn in order to equip themselves to campaign effectively and facilitate a healthy and modern democracy. Failure to grasp the implications of Obama's victory could result in electoral meltdown as other parties steal a march. Nonetheless, these lessons are ripe for misinterpretation. Some may think that the Party's task is to adopt the best ideas, practices and technologies used by Barack Obama and bolt them on to how we currently carry out party politics and campaigning. However, as Matthew McGregor argues in chapter 9, a 'build it and they will come' mentality to new campaign techniques is deeply flawed.

Instead, the facilitation of a new movement politics by the Labour Party should go deeper: it should change more fundamentally not just how the Party competes for election but also how it is organised and how it mobilises support. Thus, while Obama's election provides opportunities for Labour, it also poses a huge challenge to which the Party must respond. It depends on fully exorcising the ghost of the self-destructive indiscipline of the 1980s, the memory of which has driven a command and control approach to all aspects of party campaigns and organisation. Labour must also unlearn several of the techniques which were successful in the early years of 24/7 media in the 1990s but which are now inappropriate and counterproductive, as we enter a new age of fragmented and personalised news consumption.

Some will contend that letting go of the top down model will end in disaster, with a return to the internecine warfare of the past. But Obama showed that a successful campaign requires a mixture of a centrally managed core message alongside decentralised tools of self-organisation and a culture where it is OK to openly challenge policy and strategy. If Labour proves unwilling or unable to make the leap required, it risks ceding its role as probably the most potent weapon progressives have to achieve political change. If it cannot open up, it will become disconnected from new political movements and organisations. To understand how Labour can meet these challenges, we must first understand how it got to where it is today.

The three ages of the post-war Labour Party

The political historian Kevin Jeffreys has written that, "The Attlee era was the closest Labour ever came to becoming a mass movement, but even at this pinnacle it represented only a small fraction of the Party's electorate."[1] While this may have been the case, it is also important to note that the Labour Party of the 1950s had a strong relationship with the lifestyles, associations and rhythms of British life. This cannot not be said of any modern political party in the UK. With the exception of a brief uptick in the early Blair era, Labour Party membership has been in decline for many years. While some constituency associations remain a vibrant focal point of community action, there are many others – particularly where there is no MP or council leader to rally behind – that lack either the personnel or the financial resources to function effectively. Meanwhile, the national organisation has become a professionalised election-winning machine, favouring command and control over participatory politics.

Some choose to blame the New Labour project for the declining energy among the base but while this argument offers a comfortingly simple explanation, and correspondingly simple answer, to the Party's current predicament, it is dangerously reductionist and ahistorical. Firstly, declining membership is a 50 year-old phenomenon. In 1952, Labour had more than one million members above and beyond union affiliates.[2] Political parties during this period were successful because their organisational structures reflected the lives of the membership and offered an expression of social solidarity. Branches and constituency parties were firmly grounded in localities, and would thus encompass family, friends, neighbours and colleagues. Labour and Working Men's Clubs were linked to a local party and acted as important social hubs. In the early 1950s, the glue that held the Party together was not a rigid ideology or worldview, but instead a set of shared values and aspirations held by a broad community of supporters.

By the 1980s, the Party had a membership of fewer than 300,000 people. This decline was driven by social change as class de-alignment occurred. This reflected a more fragmented society where social solidarity was breaking down. As a result, identity became more complex and social networks more geographically disparate. This degraded the social glue that had held the Party together. Furthermore, in the age of home entertainment, the social benefits that once tempted people to join Labour were simply no longer an enticement.

The decline in membership fundamentally altered the character of the Party and was one of the root causes of the near-civil war which Labour underwent in the early 80s. The members that remained were more likely to view the world through an ideological prism, and adopt positions at odds with the Party's leadership and, more seriously, with the public. This situation was exacerbated by the creation of the Social Democratic Party in 1981. Furthermore, declining membership left Labour prone to entryism, with organisations from the hard left – which Labour had kept at arms length since its foundation – able to get their members to join failing constituency parties, and to usurp their role within Labour's decision-making apparatus. Power within Labour became uneasily suspended between the Parliamentary Labour Party and the shadow cabinet on the one hand, and the National Executive Committee, constituency parties, and conference on the other – a two-headed hydra that pulled the Labour movement in different directions. The fissure in leadership led to the drafting of the disastrous 1983 manifesto and Labour's subsequent electoral meltdown.

Since political parties' principal motivation is to win power and change society according to their view of the common good, this situation was unsustainable. Gradually, Labour 'modernisers' – first Neil Kinnock, then John Smith and subsequently Tony Blair and Gordon Brown – remodelled the Party. They did this by concentrating power in the hands of the parliamentary leadership, making the whole operation far more professional and well managed, and rebranding the Party as 'New Labour.'

This approach to politics had a considerable upside: three election victories, two of them landslides, and a period of unprecedented success. The Conservative Party, the most potent election winning force in Western Europe, was cowed to an unprecedented degree. Indeed, for a short period during the early years of Tony Blair's leadership, Labour's renewed electability led to an increase in Party membership. But there were ultimately big downsides. It created a culture of centralised politics at the heart of Labour. Scarred by the experiences of the 1980s the leadership became deeply fearful of ceding power to the grassroots, who they felt could be recaptured by the hard left. In turn, members felt disempowered and isolated from a Party elite that seemed increasingly distant. These developments created a paradox: while the organisational ideology of New Labour can be seen as a rational response to membership decline, it also became a cause of it. By 2007, the Party was down to 182,000 members.

Rethinking the logic of collective action

Participation is a good thing. But in order to generate engagement in the 21st century – and reap all the political and civic rewards that come with it – Labour must seriously consider the forms of its organisation. The Obama campaign demonstrates that generating more participation is possible today if parties adapt to the new social and technological reality and are driven by a singular theme. Although Bush's failures and Obama's positive message was critical, participation on this scale is not a uniquely American phenomenon. In the United Kingdom, campaigns such as Make Poverty History have managed to engage millions of people. These successes are not coincidental. Modern American electoral campaigns share many characteristics with civil society and pressure groups, and are what political scientist Andrew Chadwick terms hybrid organisations – part party, part movement.[3] As yet, British parties have failed to achieve such a transformation partly because they still function within institutional arrangements created in the 20th century.

The institutions that are necessary for new forms of campaign organisation have a number of distinct characteristics:

- They lack rigid institutions or overly hierarchical structures;

- They have a high level of internal pluralism;

- They have the lowest barriers to entry possible;

- They allow for multifaceted forms of participation among supporters;

- They have the ability to act as a platform on which motivated individuals and groups can self-organise;

- They are capable of interacting with other groups in the broader political eco-system.

These characteristics, alongside a singular and focused message, are shared by many successful modern political organisations. The great achievement of the Obama campaign was to take this model of activism and employ it to achieve electoral success, first in defeating the 'inevitable' candidacy of Hillary Clinton and then winning a popular majority in the presidential elections, the first time a Democratic candidate had achieved this feat in over 30 years.

How was this achieved? In a similar way to New Labour in the 1990s, the Obama campaign centralised its message. A narrative of 'hope' and 'change' – adjectives that the candidate himself embodied – was chosen at an early stage, and maintained with discipline and fervour, as David Lammy describes. Little expense was spared in achieving effective branding and cultivating an image of professionalism. The Obama team also excelled in data management, ruthlessly harvesting readily available information about their supporters as the insights offered by Yair Ghitza and Todd Rogers show. This data was used to construct a personal relationship with each individual, based on their interests, networks and willingness to work for the campaign. Additionally, Karin Christiansen and Marcus Roberts prove that training in effective campaigning techniques, such as canvassing and fundraising, was a hugely effective political weapon. This approach ensured that supporters were effectively managed and galvanised, and that the campaign was able to wring them for every last donation and hour of volunteering.

In contrast to Labour's recent history, however, the Obama team decentralised many other aspects of the campaign, and gave citizens a huge amount of freedom to self-organise. Here, the internet proved to be a vital tool. In particular, Barack Obama's web site contained a social networking element, my.barackobama.com, or MyBO as it became known. This allowed users to register with the campaign, and then create policy or interest groups with like-minded supporters (such as Veterans for Obama), organise their own fundraising drives or canvassing events, and advocate their beliefs through blogs or online petitions. This approach was extremely successful. For example, MyBO was used to organise 200,000 campaign events in communities across the country. These meetings did not come about because they were organised centrally or even planned by a local committee, but instead because self motivated citizens used tools provided by the campaign to organise themselves.

This approach to politics did not just exist in the online space. It was practiced at the community level too. As one volunteer in Ohio explained:

> "It's about empowering... we turn them around and say, 'Well hey, here's how to be a community organiser. Let me help you be a community organiser.' And then they go out and they get people to be their coordinators. And then we tell those new coordinators, 'Build yourself a team and be organisers too.' There's no end to it."[4]

Unlikely as it might seem, there are strong similarities between the Obama campaign and the parties of the 1950s. Both were constructed around real world social networks and supporter interaction. The great achievement of the Obama campaign was to employ technology to galvanise the more complex, geographically dispersed social networks that western citizens inhabit in the early 21st century. For example, in a manner similar to social networking sites such as Facebook, users of MyBO could upload their personal email address books, allowing them to contact all their family and friends and ask if they too wanted to sign up to support Obama. The internet also helped to connect supporters in strongly Republican areas of the country, where Democrats had previously been too isolated to organise.

This type of campaigning holds huge potential for Labour but may appear to hold significant risks too. Many supporters would argue that decentralisation will allow interest groups to capture campaign and policy making functions, in the way that Militant did in the

1980s. But it is easy to overstate this danger since entry-ism is only possible in closed institutions that lack firm roots in the wider community. The best long term defence we have against such attacks is not to raise barriers to participation, but to lower them.

Nor should we make the mistake of thinking that dissent is always a bad thing, an institutional mindset of which, at times, Labour has been guilty. The Obama campaign demonstrated that debate on policy can occur within a campaign in a respectful and successful manner. Indeed, MyBO could be used to agitate against the candidate's positions. Most famously, this occurred when more than 23,000 supporters joined a group to protest at Obama's support for legislation that granted legal immunity to telecommunications companies that had co-operated with the Bush administration's program of wiretapping without warrants. But rather than rebuking this group of dissenters, Obama replied directly to the group online and set out his own justification. Although agreement was not reached, campaigners felt that their concerns had been heard. Furthermore, this 'revolt' included few displays of aggression or disrespect, because activists were treated like adults and, in turn, offered the same courtesy to the campaign. A few individuals who did use the web site to make inflammatory or derogatory comments were quickly rebuked – not by the upper echelons of the campaign or some anonymous moderator, but by other activists, proving that successful participatory organisations do not need to a top-down structure to manage and respond to negative content.

Labour must escape the historical frame in which debates about structure have recently occurred. The Party must no longer view organisational decisions as a choice between the fragmented chaos of the 1980s and a 1990s-style concentration of power. Instead it must look for a new configuration that recognises today's social and technological circumstances and combines the mix of the message discipline of the 1990s with the open discourse that citizens have now come to expect.

Labour has a dedicated and professional staff who work imaginatively on uncompetitive wages to make the Party an effective campaigning force. Across the country, there are thousands of volunteers who work tirelessly with little or no reward to get Labour elected and to encourage and challenge its representatives in office. But the Party has not done these supporters and employees justice and evolved to cope with new social patterns and norms. While constitutional changes have updated the Party's core ideology and voting structures, they have not addressed the evolving desire in society to combine the individual and the collective; to find solidarity and kinship at the local level, on a timetable that suits the individual. This is the great challenge the Party faces and the real lesson of the American election.

Conclusion

We would do well to remember that no political organisation has a divine right to exist. Indeed, rather like a species of animal unable to cope with a changing environment, over the centuries parties have come and gone as the political climate has changed. While social and technological revolutions offer exciting opportunities for success, they can also be very dangerous.

All British parties are still creatures of the mass media age, when news production and dissemination was concentrated in the hands of national and local newspapers and a handful of radio and TV stations. However, as this period recedes, and we move towards an era of personalised media consumption, typified by a greater number of channels, entertainment on demand, online shopping, internet dating, social networking, and home working, parties will desperately need activists to spread their message and act as advocates of their policies within communities. Yet, paradoxically, activists need political parties less than they once did. In the networked society, citizens do not require the institutional scaffolding offered by parties to engage in political activity. Anyone can set up a simple campaigning group on an issue with a few clicks of a mouse. If people share their concerns, that group may have thousands of members in just a few hours at virtually no cost.

In such an environment, the onus is on parties to make themselves attractive vehicles for political activism and to greatly broaden their appeal. To these ends, we advocate the following five principles:

1. Remove all barriers to participation

Obama's 13 million-strong email list yielded four million individual donations. By contrast, Labour Party membership fees create a barrier to entry and make it harder to regularly ask supporters for donations. The Party currently takes in £4 million a year from its membership fees and an additional £2.3 million in 'top up' donations from around 70,000 members. This is an average of roughly £20 per subscription-only member and £50 from the more generous or wealthy. By contrast, Obama raised an average of roughly $170 (£120) from each of his donors. The time has clearly come for a new approach to this critical component of being a Labour supporter.

Scrapping party subscriptions, and instead moving towards regular fundraising drives of members and the wider progressive community, would offer supporters the chance to contribute to specific issues or electoral-based campaigns. Requests for cash could be linked to particular events like the 60th anniversary of the NHS or a local election campaign. To avoid a funding cliff edge, this new model could be phased in gradually by giving new members the right to set their own subscription level (including paying nothing). Existing members could be encouraged to change their subscription fee with an assumption, but no obligation, that it would increase.

2. Enable channels for dissent and debate

There needs to be **a cultural** *Glasnost* within the Labour Party. In this instance *Glasnost* means realising that a healthy party enables constructive internal debate, diversity of views, and dissent. It means that debates are pointless if everyone agrees. Citizens need space to reflect and political parties should offer this. Labour's traditional deliberative environments, ranging from branch meetings to conference, are too closed and hierarchical to offer such a space. Citizens today have the ability to comment at any time, anywhere on anything from the news to their latest book purchase, or even to sign a Downing Street petition. Labour must develop an open environment for debate and issue-based organisation that is open to the broader population.

3. Give supporters the tools to self-organise

The digital revolution is dramatically changing citizens' expectations. The growing personalisation of media consumption indicates a move away from geographic and temporal constraints on our activities. In this era, defined by the demand for immediacy and the individualisation of experience, it is easy to see why the political environments in some constituency parties, such as overly formal General Committee meetings, often drive away new members.

Obama's campaign proved **the power of self-organisation**, and, to remain competitive, Labour must adopt this approach. Online and offline tools can help to achieve this. Labour currently has, in technical terms, some very good online tools allowing members to publish content, organise and debate ideas with each other. These, however, are kept in a password protected, mem-

bers-only 'walled garden'. As a result, they are only useful for forming networks among those who are already
members. These systems should be opened up and
developed further, to ensure that broader connections
between progressives can be formed.

Offline, this means opening up the institutions of constituency parties. Where CLPs have opened their doors to
non-members, the number of activists in election campaigns
has spiked. However, examples such as this remain the
unusual exception. A more open approach would also help
reconnect local communities by providing new, innovative
ways to bring people together under the umbrella of the
Labour Party.

4. Keep supporters better informed

Obama's campaign proved how effectively new technology can be used to create a genuine link between
leadership and activists. It is vital that Labour
improves its use of email and other information and
communication technology, such as SMS text messaging, to form **an individualised link** with every one of
its supporters. Messages should also request action
rather than providing a one-way flow of information,
as they so frequently do.

5. Reward hard work and entrepreneurialism

The efforts of individual activists need to be recognised, allowing them to progress through the echelons
of the Party and to gain more responsibility.
Additionally, the Party should consider a move
towards **open primaries for candidate selection**. This
would have two important impacts. First, it would
ensure that the decision was not made by a small body
but by everyone in the local community. Second, it
would encourage exceptional individuals who have a

background in broader public service and share Labour's values to step forward and seek office.

We do not pretend that this transition will be easy. But we are sure it is necessary. Without taking these steps there is every risk that the Labour Party as a membership organisation will come to have little, if any, relevance to the lives of British citizens.

Indeed, it seems likely that last year's US election campaign is just the start of a seismic revolution. It is quite possible that the transition to the information age will rival the development of the printing press or of industrialisation as an epoch-forming event. Yet, even within this change, there will still be constants. There will always be people who strive for a fairer society, and those who believe that we can achieve more through common endeavour than we can alone. The question is whether the Labour Party can continue to be a suitable vehicle for these political beliefs. Can we do it?

Yes, we can.

Endnotes

Chapter 1: Introuction

1   Barack Obama, "A More Perfect Union," Philadelphia, March 18, 2008, and Barack Obama, *Dreams From My Father: A Story of Race and Inheritance* (Edinburgh: Canongate, 2007).

Chapter 2: Retrospective on the election

1   Joseph Bafumi and Robert Y Shapiro, "A New Partisan Voter," *The Journal of Politics* 71, no. 1 (2008), Robert Y Shapiro and Yaeli Bloch-Elkon, "Do the Facts Speak for Themselves? Partisan Disagreement as a Challenge to Democratic Competence," *Critical Review* 20, no. 1-2 (2008), Robert Y Shapiro and Yaeli Bloch-Elkon, "Foreign Policy, Meet the People," *The National Interest* 97, no. September-October (2008).

2   Lawrence R Jacobs and Robert Y Shapiro, *Politicians Don't Pander: Political Manipulation and the Loss of Democratic Responsiveness* (Chicago, IL: University of Chicago Press, 2000), Robert Y Shapiro, "Why Respond to Polls? Public Opinion Polling and Democracy," Public Opinion Pros, November, 2004.

3   Michael P McDonald, "2008 Unofficial Voter Turnout," *United States Elections Project*, 2008.

4   Mark Blumenthal, "Mystery Pollster: Scoring the Polls," *National Journal Online*, November 12, 2008.

5   Edison Media Research and Mitofsky International, "Evaluation of Edison/Mitofsky Election System 2004" (paper presented at the Edison Media Research and Mitofsky International, January 19, 2005).

6   Anthony Corrado, Thomas E Mann, and Trevor Potter, eds., *Inside the Campaign Finance Battle: Court Testimony on the New Reform* (Washington, D.C.: Brookings, 2003).

7   Gary Langer et al., "Exit Polls: Storm of Voter Dissatisfaction Lifts Obama to an Historic Win: Battered Economy, Partisan Shift in Power and Promise of Change Lift Obama to Victory," ABC News, November 5, 2008.

Chapter 3: Gender and the election

1   Maggie Haberman, "Hill Tops Demos, GOP Tied in Knots: Nationwide Poll," *The New York Post*, December 28, 2007, 23.

2   CNN, "Results: Iowa," CNN Election Centre, 2008.

3   Pew Research Centre's Project for Excellence in Journalism, "Character and the Primaries of 2008," Pew Research Centre, May 29, 2008. Of stories, 69 per cent of Obama narratives were positive, and 67 per cent of Clinton narratives were positive. Both Democratic contenders fared much better than Republican John McCain whose coverage was 43 per cent positive.

4   Pew Research Centre's Project for Excellence in Journalism, "Character and the Primaries of 2008," 3.

5   Karen Breslau, "Hillary Tears Up: A Muskie moment, or a helpful glimpse of 'the real Hillary'?," *Newsweek*, January 7, 2008.

6   Headlines the following day included: Geoff Earle, "Hill Gets Weary & Teary – Chokes Up Amid Cam-Pain Strain," *The New York Post*, January 8, 2008, Philip Elliott, "Emotional Clinton says 'this is very personal,' voice breaking in NH remarks," Associated Press, January 8, 2008, Errol Louis, "Calculated or Not, Weepfest Won't Help Her," Daily News, January 8, 2008.

7   Craig Gordon, "Women voters held the key to Clinton's resurgence; They strongly supported her after abandoning the campaign in Iowa," *The Houston Chronicle*, January 9, 2008, A15.

8   The state exit poll data suggest that blacks favoured Obama by a factor of 7:1 across the states on average.

9   National American Election Survey, Telephone Survey (Philadelphia, PA: Annenberg Public Policy Centre, 2008).

10   National American Election Survey, Telephone Survey.

11   MSNBC, "Exit Polls" MSNBC.com, 2008.

12   CNN, "Exit Polls," CNN Election Centre, 2008.

13   CNN, "Exit Polls."

14   Pew Research Centre, "Winning the Media Campaign," *Pew Research Center's Project for Excellence in Journalism*, October 22, 2008, 23.

15   Pew Research Centre, "Winning the Media Campaign," 14-15.

16   Pew Research Centre, "Winning the Media Campaign," 21-22.

17   National American Election Survey, Telephone Survey.

18   Pew Research Centre, "Winning the Media Campaign," 22.

19   CNN, "Exit Polls."

20   CNN, "Exit Polls."

21   Erika Falk and Kate Kenski, "Sexism Versus Partisanship: A New Look at the Question of Whether America is Ready for a Woman President," *Sex Roles* 54 (2006).

Chapter 4: The power of storytelling

1   Barack Obama, "Barack Obama's Presidential Announcement, Springfield, Illinois," YouTube, 2007.

2   Barack Obama, "Transcript: Illinois Senate Candidate Barack Obama," *Washington Post*, July 27, 2004.

3   Kevin Sullivan, "US Again Hailed as 'Country of Dreams'," *Washington Post*, November 6, 2008.

4   Ethan Bronner, "For Many Abroad, an Ideal Renewed," *New York Times*, 5 November, 2008.

Chapter 7: The web 2.0 election

1   J Stromer-Galley, "Online Interaction and Why Candidates Avoid It," *Journal Of Communications* 50, no. 4 (2000).

2   Indeed, John McCain's campaign created an ad called "Celebrity", which attacked Barack Obama for being a star like Paris Hilton. This ad, an exception to the general rule that viral videos are not created by campaigns, generated enough buzz to go viral, generating 1 million views in a few weeks, Mike SooHoo, Deputy E-campaign Director for the McCain campaign, explained in an interview.

3   P Zube, "Campaigning on MySpace: Opportunity or Vulnerability in the 2008 US Primary?," in Politics: Web 2.0: An International Conference (Royal Holloway, University of London: 2008).

4   K B Marcelo and E H Kirby, "Quick Facts about US Young Voters: The Presidential Election Year 2008," Civicyouth.org, October, 2008.

5   Vote 4 Me, "Text Messaging has Mobilized Voters in Elections Around the World. Will the Once Teen-Centric Technology Change American Politics Too?," *Newsweek*, August 2, 2006.

6   Vote 4 Me, "Text Messaging has Mobilized Voters in Elections Around the World. Will the Once Teen-Centric Technology Change American Politics Too?"

7   Combined News Service, "McCain staffer suspended over Obama, pastor video," *LATimes.com*, 2008.

8   J A Vargas, "Young voters find voice on Facebook: Site's candidate groups are grass-roots politcs for the Web generation," Washingtonpost.com, February 17, 2007.

9   Vargas, "Young voters find voice on Facebook: Site's candidate groups are grass-roots politcs for the Web generation."

10 P Burrowes, "Edwards camp goes all a-twittering," *The New York Times*, April 2, 2007.

Chapter 8: Blogging the election

1 Mayhill Fowler, "Obama: No Surprise That Hard-Pressed Pennsylvanians Turn Bitter," The Huffington Post, April 11, 2008.
2 Mike Stark, "President Obama, Please Get FISA Right," my.BarackObama.com, 2008.
3 Nataniel Silver, "FiveThirtyEight.com - Home," Five ThirtyEight.com, 2008.
4 Ben Smith, "Sign of the Media Times," *Politico*, January 2, 2009.
5 Brandon Friedman, "VetVoice," VoteVets.org, 2008/2009, Kevin Grandia, "DeSmogBlog," DeSmogBlog.com, 2008/2009.

Chapter 9: The democratising force of fundraising

1 Opensecrets, "Banking on Becoming President," Opensecrets.org, 2008.
2 Federal Election Commission, "Presidential Campaign Finance," Federal Election Commission web site, 2008.
3 All numbers in this section from Jose Antonio Vargas, "Obama Raised Half a Billion Online," *Washington Post*, November 20, 2008.
4 CNN, "Clinton Outpaces Obama in Fundraising for Third Quarter," CNN.com, October 2, 2007.

Chapter 10: Data-driven politics

1 A S Gerber and D P Green, "The Effects of Canvassing, Telephone Calls, and Direct Mail on Voter Turnout: A Field Experiment," *American Political Science Review* 94, no. 3 (2000).
2 A S Gerber and D P Green, Get Out the Vote: How to Increase Vote Turnout (Washington DC: Brookings, 2008).
3 K Arceneaux and D W Nickerson, "Who is Mobilized to Vote? A Re-Analysis of Eleven Field Experiments,"

American Journal of Political Science 53, no. 1 (2009).
4   Catalist/Analyst Institute, "2008 Election Analysis," National Press Club, January 15, 2009.
5   AFL-CIO, Analyst Institute, "2008 Election Analysis."

Chapter 11: Campaigning for Congress

1   John Samples and Patrick Basham, "Once Again, Incumbents Are the Big Winners," Cato Institute, 2004.
2   Aaron Applegate, "Beach's 2nd District race shapes up to be competitive," *The Virginian-Pilot*, July 28, 2008.
3   Full details of voting records can be found at National Journal, "2007 Vote Ratings," nationaljournal.com, 2008.
4   Federal Election Commission, "House and Senate Races," Federal Election Commission web site, 2008.
5   Editorial, "For Congress: Glenn Nye," *The Virginian-Pilot*, October 24, 2008.

Chapter 12: Conclusion

1   Kevin Jefferys, Politics and the People: A History of British Democracy Since 1918 (London: Atlantic, 2007).
2   All membership data before 2000 from David Butler and Gareth Butler, *Twentieth Century British Political Facts 1900-2000* (Basingstoke: Macmillan, 2000), 151. 2007 figure from Patrick Wintour and Sarah Hall, "Labour Membership Halved," *The Guardian*, 2004.
3   Andrew Chadwick, "Digital Network Repertoires and Organizational Hybridity," *Political Communications* 24 (2007).
4   Zack Exley, "The New Organizers, Part 1: What's Really Behind Obama's Ground Game," Huffington Post, October 8, 2008.

Bibliography

A Applegate. 'Beach's 2nd District race shapes up to be competitive', in *The Virginian-Pilot* (2008). Available at: http://hamptonroads.com/2008/07/beachs-2nd-district-race-shapes-be-competitive. Accessed February 2, 2009.

K Arceneaux and D W Nickerson, 'Who is Mobilized to Vote? A Re-Analysis of Eleven Field Experiments', *American Journal of Political Science*, 53 (2009).

J Bafumi and R Y Shapiro, 'A New Partisan Voter', *The Journal of Politics*, 71 (2008), pp. 1-24.

M Blumenthal. 'Mystery Pollster: Scoring the Polls', in *National Journal Online* (2008). Available at: http://www.nationaljournal.com/njonline/mp_20081111_6722.php. Accessed February 2, 2009.

K Breslau. 'Hillary Tears Up: A Muskie moment, or a helpful glimpse of 'the real Hillary'?' in *Newsweek* (2008). Available at: http://www.newsweek.com/id/85609. Accessed February 4, 2009.

E Bronner. 'For Many Abroad, an Ideal Renewed', in *New York Times* (2008). Available at: http://www.nytimes.com/2008/11/05/us/politics/05global.html?ref=world. Accessed January 2, 2008.

P Burrowes. 'Edwards camp goes all a-twittering', in The New York Times (2007). Available at: http://www.nytimes.com/cq/2007/2004/2002/cq_2499.html?pagewanted=print. Accessed February 6, 2009.

D Butler and G Butler, *Twentieth Century British Political*

Facts 1900-2000 (Basingstoke, 2000).

Catalist / Analyst Institute. '2008 Election Analysis', in, *National Press Club*, (Washington DC, 2009).

A Chadwick, 'Digital Network Repertoires and Organizational Hybridity', *Political Communications*, 24 (2007), pp. 283-301.

CNN. 'Clinton Outpaces Obama in Fundraising for Third Quarter', in CNN.com (2007). Available at: http://www.cnn.com/2007/POLITICS/10/02/campaign.cash/index.html. Accessed 28 January, 2008.

———. 'Exit Polls', in *CNN Election Centre* (2008). Available at: http://edition.cnn.com/ELECTION/2008/results/polls/#val=USP00p1. Accessed February 4, 2009.

———. 'Results: Iowa', in *CNN Election Centre* (2008). Available at: http://edition.cnn.com/ELECTION/2008/primaries/results/state/#IA. Accessed February 4, 2009.

Combined News Service. 'McCain staffer suspended over Obama, pastor video', in LATimes.com (2008). Available at: http://www.latimes.com/news/nationworld/washingtondc/ny-uspoll215621233mar215621221,215621231,214504897.story. Accessed February 6, 2009.

A Corrado, T E Mann and T Potter, eds., *Inside the Campaign Finance Battle: Court Testimony on the New Reform* (Washington, D.C., 2003).

G Earle. 'Hill Gets Weary & Teary – Chokes Up Amid Cam-Pain Strain', in *The New York Post* (2008). Available at. Accessed

Edison Media Research and Mitofsky International. 'Evaluation of Edison/Mitofsky Election System 2004', in N. E. P. (NEP) ed., *Edison Media Research and Mitofsky International*, 2005).

Editorial. 'For Congress: Glenn Nye', in *The Virginian-Pilot* (2008). Available at: http://hamptonroads.com/2008/10/congress-glenn-nye. Accessed February 2, 2009.

P Elliott. 'Emotional Clinton says 'this is very personal,' voice breaking in NH remarks', in, *The Associated Press*, 2008).

Z Exley. 'The New Organizers, Part 1: What's Really Behind Obama's Ground Game', in Huffington Post (2008). Available at: http://www.huffingtonpost.com/zack-exley/the-new-organizers-part-1_b_132782.html. Accessed November 25, 2008.

E Falk and K Kenski, 'Sexism Versus Partisanship: A New Look at the Question of Whether America is Ready for a Woman President', *Sex Roles*, 54 (2006), pp. 413-428.

Federal Election Commission. 'House and Senate Races', in Federal Election Commission web site (2008). Available at: http://www.fec.gov/DisclosureSearch/mapHSApp.do. Accessed January 28, 2008.

———. 'Presidential Campaign Finance', in Federal Election Commission web site (2008). Available at: http://www.fec.gov/DisclosureSearch/mapApp.do?cand_id=P80003338&searchType=&searchSQLType=&searchKeyword=. Accessed January 28, 2008.

M Fowler. 'Obama: No Surprise That Hard-Pressed Pennsylvanians Turn Bitter', in The Huffington Post (2008). Available at: http://www.huffingtonpost.com/mayhill-fowler/obama-no-surprise-that-ha_b_96188.html. Accessed December 30, 2008.

B Friedman. 'VetVoice', in VoteVets.org (2008/2009). Available at: http://vetvoice.com. Accessed February 2, 2009.

A S Gerber and D P Green, *Get Out the Vote: How to Increase Vote Turnout* (Washington DC, 2008).

A S Gerber and D P Green, 'The Effects of Canvassing, Telephone Calls, and Direct Mail on Voter Turnout: A Field Experiment', *American Political Science Review*, 94 (2000).

C Gordon. 'Women voters held the key to Clinton's resurgence; They strongly supported her after abandoning the campaign in Iowa', in, *The Houston Chronicle*, 2008).

K Grandia. 'DeSmogBlog', in DeSmogBlog.com (2008/2009). Available at: http://www.desmogblog.com Accessed February 2, 2009.

M Haberman. 'Hill Tops Demos, GOP Tied in Knots:

Nationwide Poll', in, The New York Post, (New York, 2007), p. 23.

L R Jacobs and R Y Shapiro, *Politicians Don't Pander: Political Manipulation and the Loss of Democratic Responsiveness* (Chicago, IL, 2000).

K Jefferys, Politics and the People: *A History of British Democracy Since 1918* (London, 2007).

G Langer, R Morin, B Hartman, P Craighill, C Deane, M Brodie, P Moynihan, B Shapiro and S Clement. 'Exit Polls: Storm of Voter Dissatisfaction Lifts Obama to an Historic Win: Battered Economy, Partisan Shift in Power and Promise of Change Lift Obama to Victory', in ABC News (2008). Available at: http://abcnews.go.com/ PollingUnit/Vote2008/story?id=6189129&page=1. Accessed February 2, 2009.

E Louis. 'Calculated or Not, Weepfest Won't Help Her', in, *Daily News*, 2008), p. 6.

K B Marcelo and E H Kirby. 'Quick Facts about US Young Voters: The Presidential Election Year 2008', in Civicyouth.org (2008). Available at: http://www.civic youth.org/PopUps/FS_08_quick_facts_national.pdf. Accessed February 9, 2009.

M P McDonald. '2008 Unofficial Voter Turnout', in *United States Elections Project* (2008). Available at: http://elections. gmu.edu/preliminary_vote_2008.html. Accessed February 2, 2009.

National American Election Survey, *Telephone Survey* (Philadelphia, PA, 2008).

National Journal. '2007 Vote Ratings', in nationaljournal.com (2008). Available at: http:// www.nationaljournal.com/voteratings/. Accessed February 2, 2009.

B Obama. 'Transcript: Illinois Senate Candidate Barack Obama', in *Washington Post* (2004). Available at: http://www.washingtonpost.com/wp-dyn/ articles/A19751-2004Jul27.html. Accessed January 2, 2009.

———. 'Barack Obama's Presidential Announcement,

Springfield, Illinois', in YouTube (2007). Available at: http://uk.youtube.com/watch?v=gdJ7Ad15WCA. Accessed December 22.

———, *Dreams From My Father: A Story of Race and Inheritance* (Edinburgh, 2007).

———. 'A More Perfect Union', in *Philadelphia* (2008). Available at: http://my.barackobama.com/page/content/hisownwords. Accessed February 4, 2009.

Opensecrets. 'Banking on Becoming President', in Opensecrets.org (2008). Available at: http://www.open secrets.org/pres08/index.php. Accessed January 28, 2008.

Pew Research Centre's Project for Excellence in Journalism. 'Character and the Primaries of 2008', in *Pew Research Centre* (2008). Available at: http://journalism.org/node/11266. Accessed February 4, 2009.

Pew Research Centre. 'Winning the Media Campaign', in *Pew Research Center's Project for Excellence in Journalism* (2008). Available at: http://journalism.org/node/13307. Accessed February 4, 2009.

J Samples and P Basham. 'Once Again, Incumbents Are the Big Winners', in *Cato Institute* (2004). Available at: http://www.cato.org/pub_display.php?pub_id=2889. Accessed February 2, 2009.

R Y Shapiro. 'Why Respond to Polls? Public Opinion Polling and Democracy', in *Public Opinion Pros* (2004). Available at: http://www.publicopinionpros.com/features/2004/nov/shapiro.htm. Accessed November 22, 2008.

R Y Shapiro and Y Bloch-Elkon, 'Do the Facts Speak for Themselves? Partisan Disagreement as a Challenge to Democratic Competence', *Critical Review*, 20 (2008), pp. 115-139.

———, 'Foreign Policy, Meet the People', *The National Interest*, 97 (2008), pp. 37-43.

N Silver. 'FiveThirtyEight.com – Home', in FiveThirty Eight.com (2008). Available at: http://www.fivethirty eight.com/2008/03/frequently-asked-questions-last-revised.html. Accessed December 30, 2008.

B Smith. 'Sign of the Media Times', in *Politico* (2009). Available at: http://www.politico.com/blogs/bensmith/0109/Sign_of_the_media_times.html?showall. Accessed February 2, 2008.

M Stark. 'President Obama, Please Get FISA Right', in my.BarackObama.com (2008). Available at: http://my.barackobama.com/page/group/Senator Obama-PleaseVoteAgainstFISA. Accessed December 30, 2008.

J Stromer-Galley, 'Online Interaction and Why Candidates Avoid It', *Journal Of Communications*, 50 (2000), pp. 111-132.

K Sullivan. 'US Again Hailed as 'Country of Dreams'', in *Washington Post* (2008). Available at: http://www.washingtonpost.com/wp-dyn/content/story/2008/11/06/ST2008110600708.html. Accessed January 2, 2008.

J A Vargas. 'Young voters find voice on Facebook: Site's candidate groups are grass-roots politics for the Web generation', in Washingtonpost.com (2007). Available at: http://www.washingtonpost.com/wp-dyn/content/article/2007/2002/2016/AR2007021602084_pf.html. Accessed February 5, 2009.

————. 'Obama Raised Half a Billion Online', in *Washington Post* (2008). Available at: http://voices.washingtonpost.com/the-trail/2008/11/20/obama_raised_half_a_billion_on.html. Accessed December 4, 2008.

Vote 4 Me. 'Text Messaging has Mobilized Voters in Elections Around the World. Will the Once Teen-Centric Technology Change American Politics Too?' in *Newsweek* (2006). Available at: http://www.newsweek.com/id/46675/page/46671. Accessed February 6, 2009.

P Wintour and S Hall. 'Labour Membership Halved', in *The Guardian* (2004). Available at: http://politics.guardian.co.uk/labour/story/0,9061,1274855,00.html. Accessed February 22, 2008.

P Zube. 'Campaigning on MySpace: Opportunity or Vulnerability in the 2008 US Primary?' in, Politics: Web 2.0: An International Conference, (Royal Holloway, University of London, 2008).

The Fabian Review, 2008

British Muslims and the politics of fairness

In 'Fairness not Favours', Sadiq Khan MP argues that an effective agenda to provide opportunity and tackle extremism across all communities must go beyond a narrow approach to security, and sets out new proposals for a progressive agenda on inequality and life chances, public engagement in foreign policy, an inclusive Britishness, and rethinking the role of faith in public life.

The pamphlet puts the case for an effective agenda to provide opportunity and tackle extremism across all communities must go beyond a narrow approach to security, and sets out new proposals for a progressive agenda on inequality and life chances, public engagement in foreign policy, an inclusive Britishness, and rethinking the role of faith in public life.

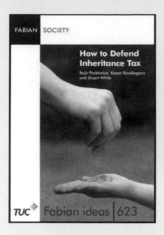

How to defend inheritance tax

Inheritance tax is under attack, and not just from the political right. The critics of this tax have dominated the debate over recent years but, as the authors of 'How to Defend Inheritance Tax' argue, this tax is one of the best tools we have for tackling inequality and kick starting Britain's stalled social mobility.

Defending inheritance tax is not just the responsibility of politicians – there must be a citizen-led campaign too. In this Fabian Ideas pamphlet, **Rajiv Prabhakar, Karen Rowlingson and Stuart White** provide progressives with the tools they need to win this argument.

They set out the evidence on inheritance and inequality, tackle the common objections to the tax, and demonstrate the moral and pragmatic arguments for an inheritance tax.

'The Fabians ask the most difficult questions, pushing Labour to make a bold, progressive case on taxation and the abolition of child poverty.'
– **Polly Toynbee**

How to narrow the gap and tackle child poverty

One in five children still grows up in poverty in Britain. Yet all the political parties now claim to care about 'social justice'. This report sets a litmus test by which Brown, Cameron and Campbell must be judged.

'Narrowing the Gap' is the final report of the Fabian Commission on Life Chances and Child Poverty, chaired by Lord Victor Adebowale. The Fabian Society is the only think tank with members. Join us and help us put poverty and equality at the centre of the political agenda.

JOIN THE FABIANS TODAY
Join us and receive two Fabian Reviews, plus our award-winning equality report, 'Narrowing the Gap'

I'd like to become a Fabian for just £9.95

I understand that should at any time during my six-month introductory membership period I wish to cancel, I will receive a refund and keep all publications received without obligation. After six months I understand my membership will revert to the annual rate as published in *Fabian Review*, currently £33 (ordinary) or £16 (unwaged).

Name

Date of birth

Address

Postcode

Email

Telephone

Instruction to Bank   Originator's ID: 971666

Bank/building society name

DIRECT Debit

Address

Postcode

Acct holder(s)

Acct no.

Sort code

I instruct you to pay direct debits from my account at the request of the Fabian Society. The instruction is subject to the safeguards of the Direct Debit Guarantee.

Signature

Date

Return to:
Fabian Society Membership
FREEPOST SW 1570
11 Dartmouth Street, London SW1H 9BN